Indicators of Precollege Education in Science and Mathematics

A Preliminary Review

Senta A. Raizen and
Lyle V. Jones, editors

Committee on Indicators of Precollege
Science and Mathematics Education

Commission on Behavioral and
Social Sciences and Education

National Research Council

National Academy Press
Washington, D.C. 1985

National Academy Press 2101 Constitution Avenue, NW Washington, DC 20418

NOTICE: The project that is the subject of this report was approved by the Governing Board of the National Research Council, whose members are drawn from the councils of the National Academy of Sciences, the National Academy of Engineering, and the Institute of Medicine. The members of the committee responsible for the report were chosen for their special competences and with regard for appropriate balance.

This report has been reviewed by a group other than the authors according to procedures approved by a Report Review Committee consisting of members of the National Academy of Sciences, the National Academy of Engineering, and the Institute of Medicine.

The National Research Council was established by the National Academy of Sciences in 1916 to associate the broad community of science and technology with the Academy's purposes of furthering knowledge and of advising the federal government. The Council operates in accordance with general policies determined by the Academy under the authority of its congressional charter of 1863, which establishes the Academy as a private nonprofit, self-governing membership corporation. The Council has become the principal operating agency of both the National Academy of Sciences and the National Academy of Engineering in the conduct of their services to the government, the public, and the scientific and engineering communities. It is administered jointly by both Academies and the Institute of Medicine. The National Academy of Engineering and the Institute of Medicine were established in 1964 and 1970, respectively, under the charter of the National Academy of Sciences.

This study by a committee of the National Research Council (NRC) was supported by the NRC Fund, which consists of contributions from: a consortium of private foundations including the Carnegie Corporation of New York, the Charles E. Culpeper Foundation, the William and Flora Hewlett Foundation, and John D. and Catherine T. MacArthur Foundation, the Andrew W. Mellon Foundation, the Rockefeller Foundation, and Alfred P. Sloan Foundation; the Academy Industry Program, which seeks annual contributions from companies that are concerned with the health of U.S. science and technology and with public policy issues with technological content; and the endowments of the National Academy of Sciences and the National Academy of Engineering.

Library of Congress Cataloging in Publication Data
Main entry under title:

Indicators of precollege education in science and mathematics.

Bibliography: p.

1. Science — Study and teaching (Secondary) — United States — Evaluation. 2. Mathematics — Study and teaching (Secondary) — United States — Evaluation. 3. Science indicators — United States. I. Raizen, Senta A. II. Jones, Lyle V. III. National Research Council (U.S.). Committee on Indicators of Precollege Science and Mathematics Education.

Q183.3.A.1I53 1985 507'.1073 85-3028

International Standard Book Number 0-309-03536-8

Printed in the United States of America

Committee on Indicators of Precollege Science and Mathematics Education

LYLE V. JONES *(Chair)*, L. L. Thurstone Psychometric Laboratory, University of North Carolina (psychology, statistics)
RICHARD D. ANDERSON, Council of Scientific Societies Presidents, Washington, D.C. (mathematics)
NORMAN M. BRADBURN, Provost, University of Chicago (survey research)
DENIS F. JOHNSTON, Washington, D.C. (statistics, social indicators)
C. THOMAS KERINS, Illinois Office of Education, Springfield (program evaluation and testing)
HAROLD NISSELSON, Westat, Inc., Rockville, Maryland (statistics)
DONALD B. RUBIN, Departments of Statistics and Education, University of Chicago (statistics)
MARSHALL S. SMITH, Wisconsin Center for Education Research, University of Wisconsin (educational research and policy)
MARY L. TENOPYR, AT&T, New York, N.Y. (industrial psychology)
WAYNE W. WELCH, Department of Education, University of Minnesota (educational psychology, science education)

SENTA A. RAIZEN, *Study Director*

Preface

Some 25 years ago, in the wake of the launching of Sputnik by the Soviet Union, the United States embarked on a reform of science and mathematics education. The primary objective then was to ensure that a sizable number of students would be motivated to choose scientific and technical careers and would be well educated to do so. Today, again, the United States is embarking on a reform of science and mathematics education. But the present call for reform embraces a larger mission: not only to meet the country's need for scientific and technical manpower, but also to ensure scientific and technical literacy for all students. Students must be prepared for the changing requirements of a society more and more heavily linked to rapidly advancing technology, no matter at what stage they terminate formal education.

To help assess the degree to which this ambitious new goal is approached, the National Research Council established a Committee on Indicators of Precollege Science and Mathematics Education. Many efforts are already under way to improve the teaching and learning of mathematics and science by all students in elementary and secondary school. To understand the impact of these efforts and make them more effective in the future, it is important to be able to monitor the condition of science and mathematics education in the nation's schools. And for that monitoring, assessment measures—indicators—must be available. The committee was charged with developing a framework for an efficient set of indicators, filling in the framework as far as possible with existing data to provide a baseline, and suggesting what data and analyses will be needed in the future for a continuing portrayal of the condition of precollege science and mathematics education.

This report presents the committee's work, based on a review of information and data currently available. As the title of the report indicates, it is a preliminary study, but we hope one that lays a solid foundation for the next tasks, to be performed by a successor committee that will include mathematicians and scientists as well as experts in educational research and data. Under the chairmanship of John G. Truxal, Department of Technology and Sociology, State University of New York at Stony Brook, the successor committee will address the important goal of developing imaginative new indicators. It will also continue to consult with state departments of education and will initiate communication with local school districts to help build a coordinated monitoring system for mathematics and science education. The new committee will be helped in its work by other National Research Council activities, for example, the Committee on Research in Mathematics, Science, and Technology Education, which is examining what research needs to be done to address critical substantive issues pertaining to the improvement of mathematics and science education.

We wish to acknowledge the assistance provided to our committee by a number of state officials; their names are listed in the Appendix. As the work of the successor committee proceeds, the help of state and local education authorities will continue to be needed to bring about a monitoring system for science and mathematics education that is useful at all levels of educational governance.

The committee extends to Senta A. Raizen, study director, its greatest expression of gratitude: without her initiative, perseverance, and enthusiastic dedication to our task, this report could not have been written.

LYLE V. JONES, *Chair*
Committee on Indicators of
Precollege Science and Mathematics
Education

Contents

1
Introduction and Summary

INTRODUCTION

Background

In the last 2 years, concern over the state of science and mathematics education in the schools of the United States has become a prominent topic on the public agenda. Special commissions and task forces have emphasized the importance to the nation of adequate student preparation in science and mathematics. For example, the National Science Board Commission on Precollege Education in Mathematics, Science and Technology (National Science Foundation, 1983:1) states that "improved preparation of all students in the fields of mathematics, science and technology is essential to the maintenance and development of our Nation's economic strength, to its military security, to its commitment to the democratic ideal of an informed and participating citizenry and to fulfilling personal lives for its people." The Task Force on Education for Economic Growth (1983) in the report Action for Excellence views the declining exposure of students to technical subjects as a serious problem that threatens to become more so as American workers face increasing technological demands. The Report of the Twentieth Century Fund Task Force on Federal Elementary and Secondary Education Policy (1983) presents the view that training in mathematics and science is critical to both the nation's economy and polity--to the economy by ensuring that there are ample personnel who are capable of filling the increasing number of jobs demanding these skills, and to the polity by providing citizens with the education in science that is essential if they are to participate intelligently in political decisions about such controversial issues as radiation, pollution, and nuclear energy. The National Commission on Excellence in Education (1983) recommends that schooling now include "five new basics": in addition to 4 years of English and 3 years of social studies, all high school students should study no less than 3 years of mathematics, 3 years of science, and 1/2 year of computer science.

These national bodies, convened with private or governmental sponsorship, agree that there are serious problems in precollege mathematics and science education and that those problems may constitute a threat to the economic future and to the security of our nation. Other groups, sponsored by a number of states, have reached similar conclusions. The reports suggest that many U.S. students are leaving high school without adequate preparation in science and mathematics, whether for the job market or for continuing their education. The reports also identify specific school deficiencies: teacher shortages, inadequate curricula, low standards of student performance.

According to some critics (see, for example, Peterson, 1983; Stedman and Smith, 1983), however, not all of the conclusions of the national commissions are adequately documented. Yet the expressed concerns about deficiencies already have led to initiatives by government and by the private sector at the national, state, and local levels. Legislation passed by Congress in 1983 made available funds to the National Science Foundation to be invested specifically in training mathematics and science teachers and in providing improved instruction in these fields, and there were further congressional appropriations in 1984. More than 40 states either have increased high school graduation requirements in mathematics and science or are considering an increase in requirements (Education Commission of the States, 1983). University systems in several states have announced higher admission requirements. State and local initiatives provide in-service education in mathematics or science for teachers already practicing and encourage college students to embark on careers in mathematics or science teaching. Private corporations are donating equipment, providing training and research experiences for teachers and students, and lending staff members to the schools for special programs.

The renewed interest and investment in precollege mathematics and science education make it especially important to understand the current condition of these fields and to be able to track future changes. Two major reports on education released recently have urged that educational progress be systematically monitored. The National Science Board Commission (National Science Foundation, 1983:12) recommends:

> The Federal government should finance and maintain a national mechanism to measure student achievement and participation in a manner that allows national, state and local evaluation and comparison of educational progress . . . [an] assessment mechanism is needed to enable local communities, States and the Nation to monitor their progress toward improving mathematics, science and technology skills among elementary and secondary students and to incorporate such information into their program development activities. . . . The Commission firmly believes that achieving its educational objectives requires regular monitoring of educational progress, and that such monitoring will itself increase the speed of change.

The report of the Carnegie Foundation for the Advancement of Teaching (Boyer, 1983) recommends that new student achievement tests be developed. They would be linked to the content of the high school curriculum and would be given to all students toward the end of high school to evaluate what students have learned.

Even before the issuance of these reports, the National Academy of Sciences and the National Academy of Engineering (1982) had expressed concern about the status of precollege science and mathematics education and also about the facilities available for monitoring the nation's educational progress. A national convocation on precollege science and mathematics education held by the Academies drew attention not only to the problems but also to the lack of adequate information regarding teachers, enrollments, and other important issues.

To lay the foundation for the development of a monitoring system for use at the national, state, and local levels, the Committee on Indicators of Precollege Science and Mathematics Education was created in 1983. The committee is charged with proposing a framework for an efficient set of education indicators, filling in the framework to the extent possible with existing data, and suggesting data and data analyses that will be needed in the future for a continuing portrayal of the condition of precollege science and mathematics education. This report covers the first phase of the committee's work.

Scope of Report

In the work discussed in this report, the committee selected a preliminary set of indicators, based on the kind of information that is generally requested by people making decisions about education and on which some data have been collected. The committee also reviewed the information currently available on selected indicators and has provided some findings on temporal trends and comparisons with other countries. Lastly, the committee has judged the extent to which the available information can serve to construct indicators and has made recommendations for improvement.

This report is a preliminary statement rather than a definitive document on indicators. It represents a first attempt to select indicators of precollege mathematics and science education that might be constructed over the short range and presents the committee's recommendations for improving the information pertinent to the selected indicators. The report is addressed primarily to the agencies that are most likely to develop and publish education indicators for science and mathematics, the National Science Foundation, the National Center for Education Statistics, the National Institute of Education, the International Association for the Evaluation of Educational Achievement, as well as to state and local offices of education. It is also addressed to a wider audience of educators, educational researchers, scientists and mathematicians, with the intent of stimulating critical comment that may help to advise those agencies.

This report has several limitations. The committee was asked to prepare a preliminary report promptly. Both the shortness of time and budgetary restrictions placed constraints on its work. As a consequence, the committee chose to restrict its scope to indicators that can be constructed from information already being collected at the national, state, or local levels or that could be collected by a modest extension of present data collection activities.

In this report the committee summarizes conclusions and makes recommendations regarding the quality of available information and its suitability for the selected indicators. The committee also derives from the data some findings about the current condition of science and mathematics education. In its interpretation of cited studies, the committee routinely has focused only on statistically significant results as indicated by the standard errors reported in the original sources.

The committee does not provide value judgments about the findings derived from the studies and data cited. It is the committee's view that such judgments should be made by educators, scientists, legislators, school boards, parents--all those concerned with the quality of education in this country--based on a clear understanding of current conditions and trends. The report tries to further this understanding; it is not intended to be a certificate of health or a report card on the nation's mathematics and science education.

The committee makes no attempt in this report to investigate underlying causes of the observed conditions. Effective education policy requires, first, an understanding of current conditions, second, a definition of preferred conditions, and, third, an appreciation of means for changing current to preferred conditions, which in turn requires an understanding of their causes. This preliminary report deals only with a portrayal of current conditions; it does not define preferred conditions, nor does it discuss how changes leading to the preferred conditions might be brought about.

When projections about conditions over the next several years are given, as in the section on teachers, they are based on extrapolations of current modes of school operation and on predictable changes such as demographic trends. Possible structural reforms of the present system, for example, that might accompany the application of information technology to education, or major alterations in the school curriculum with respect to the content and sequencing of mathematics, science, and perhaps newly added technology instruction, would alter the projections.

Logical next steps in the development of an adequate monitoring system would entail considering more imaginative and less conventional indicators that might serve to guide policy for mathematics and science education, considering indicators that might be useful in the context of possible changes of structure or function in the education delivery system, and, of course, designing better data gathering methods and analyses for all indicators. In the next phase of the work, these objectives will be addressed.

SUMMARY

The first section of this summary presents a short discussion, given in greater detail in Chapter 2, of the reasons for choosing particular schooling variables as the basis for constructing indicators. Subsequent sections of the summary provide the committee's findings, conclusions, and recommendations on the selected indicators related to teachers, curriculum content, instructional time and course enrollment, and student achievement in science and mathematics.

Selecting Indicators

A large amount of statistical data and research information on education in general is available. At the national level, the National Center for Education Statistics (NCES), a component of the Department of Education, publishes two major compilations annually. The NCES and other components of the Department also sponsor periodic surveys--for example, the National Longitudinal Study of 1972 (NLS 1972) high school graduates and High School and Beyond Study (HSB), a survey of 1980 sophomores and seniors and 1982 seniors--that provide information on student enrollment and achievement, although information specific to mathematics and science education is limited. The Department, through the National Institute of Education, also supports the National Assessment of Educational Progress (NAEP), which has gathered information nationwide on scholastic achievement (including mathematics and science achievement) and student attitudes since 1969. The National Science Foundation (NSF) has special responsibility in the area of science and mathematics education: it has sponsored studies on science and mathematics in the schools and published information from them and other sources. Both NCES and NSF have provided support for U.S. participation in the studies conducted by the International Association for Evaluation of Educational Achievement (IEA).

Every state also has its own data collection system, much of it devoted to fiscal, demographic, and managerial information, but also including data on enrollments, personnel, and student assessment, although there is considerable variation in the types of data collected by states and in the manner of collection. (Examples of the types of data collected by states are given in the

Appendix.) The larger local education districts similarly collect information they find necessary for their internal operation as well as data requested by the state agencies. Information systems of local education districts exhibit an even greater diversity than those of the state systems.

Thus, considerable data are available on precollege science and mathematics education, but they are derived from diverse sources, address similar questions differently, and leave some pertinent issues unaddressed. To begin the development of an orderly monitoring system, the committee's first task was to select a limited set of variables and measures deemed essential to portraying the state of science and mathematics education. The committee chose to concentrate on variables generally identified as critical to the condition of education and on which there were some data and information available. The outcomes of science and mathematics education were considered first, followed by the schooling processes and inputs that can be associated with the selected outcomes.

Outcome Variables

The primary goal of instruction in science and mathematics is student learning. The most explicit student outcome, and one that can be tied directly to schooling variables, is the knowledge and skills gained by students, that is, student achievement in science and mathematics. Hence, the first, most obvious outcome variable the committee selected is student achievement.

A second outcome often desired from instruction in these fields is the development of more favorable student attitudes toward science and mathematics. At this time the committee is not giving emphasis to indicators on attitudinal variables because their relationship to the primary goal of student achievement (or to later-life outcomes) is not clear. Other outcomes considered by the committee included choice of college majors, choice of careers, and later career paths. Each of these is important to individual and societal goals and is relevant to the distribution of human resources. However, the more distant an outcome from the immediate purpose of instruction, the more tenuous the link and the more likely that nonschool variables affect the outcome. Pending research findings that more clearly link school experiences to life outcomes, the committee did not chose indicators representing such outcomes.

As to measures of achievement, the only ones available at the national level that are applicable to the whole student population are test results from NAEP, NLS, and HSB. The committee does not believe that the scores obtained on the Scholastic Aptitude Tests (SATs) developed by Educational Testing Service (ETS) are appropriate measures of school outcomes for all students in science and mathematics, because the population taking these tests is self-selected and not representative of the whole student population. However, for college-bound students who take them, trends in scores on the achievement tests in specific subjects also developed by ETS for the College Board's Admission Testing Program and the tests of the American College Testing Program give an indication of changing levels of achievement over time in academic subjects offered in high school.

From time to time studies of school achievement in various countries are carried out. The most comprehensive of these have been the studies conducted under the auspices of the IEA. However, the most widely published results for mathematics date back to 1964 and for science to 1970. New IEA studies are currently under way in both fields, and some preliminary results from these studies are available.

Most states have assessment programs as well, although they vary from state to state; they generally involve selective achievement testing at several grade levels, sometimes using commercial tests, sometimes state-constructed instruments. State tests are used for a variety of purposes: for assessing absolute achievement, for determining competency, for comparison with national results, for comparison of schools and school districts, for checking on the adequacy of curricula and instruction. Some of these purposes require periodic adjustment of the tests, which makes comparisons over time hazardous.

Using test scores as measures of student achievement assumes at least moderate test validity for the assessment of student learning. Unfortunately, it has proved difficult with current testing methodology to construct tests for widespread use that adequately asses the range of complex skills and in-depth understanding needed for proficiency in mathematical or scientific concepts and processes. The committee, in its recommendations, discusses the importance of improving tests, especially for testing the knowledge and skills acquired by individuals. Nevertheless, the committee has concluded that existing tests of mathematics and science of the kinds used by

NAEP, HSB, and IEA are sufficiently valid for the purpose of indicating student achievement at the group level.

Process Variables

The selection of student achievement as the outcome variable of greatest interest determines to a considerable extent what schooling input and process variables need to be selected, namely, those that have some causal relationship to student achievement. One process variable in particular is assumed in educational practice to be closely linked to student achievement: enrollment in or instructional time spent on the requisite subject. And recent work on the achievement of high school students in mathematics and in science documents the positive effects of time spent on relevant instruction or courses, especially if instructional time is managed efficiently; in fact, it appears to be one of the most robust findings coming from major longitudinal studies and assessment efforts. Consequently, based on research evidence as well as on educational practice and experience, the committee decided that course enrollment and instructional time spent on subject matter should be considered key process variables in indicators of mathematics and science education. A related exposure component is time spent on homework, which appears to be associated with student achievement, and it is included as part of these process variables.

Selection of course enrollment and instructional time in no way is intended to minimize the importance of such other process variables as teacher behaviors, student behaviors, and classroom environment, but because of the present state of knowledge about the relationships between these variables and student achievement and about how to assess them, the committee decided it would be premature to use them at this time as indicators of mathematics and science education.

Input Variables

In addition to outcome and process variables, a third set of variables in measuring science and mathematics education are schooling inputs. The most obvious inputs are numbers (and quality) of teachers responsible for those areas of instruction and the content of the curriculum.

Looking first at the numbers of mathematics and science teachers, reasonably consistent statistics are available from NCES and the National Science Teachers Association. However, the significant indicator is not the supply of teachers, but the supply compared with the numbers needed; this comparison must be based not only on the size of the existing pool, but also on the teacher turnover rate, total high school enrollments, and the effects of increased high school graduation requirements that are being mandated by a number of states. But even good estimates of the numbers of teachers do not take into account quality, the competence of either those teachers now assigned to mathematics and science classes or of those entering the fields.

There is no nationally accepted standard for a "qualified" science or mathematics teacher. While certification can be used as a first approximation of quality, certification requirements vary considerably from state to state. Hence, estimates of the numbers of qualified people teaching mathematics or science are open to question. In spite of these difficulties in measuring the supply and quality of teachers, however, the committee decided that their importance warranted selecting them as variables.

The argument for selecting content of curriculum as a variable is analogous to that for selecting instructional time/course enrollment: the subject matter actually taught is important to student achievement. Recent syntheses of the sizable research literature on the efficacy of alternative science curricula and data from NAEP and HSB support this assumption. It should be noted that, of the variables the committee considered it important to assess, this one has received the least attention, probably because it is the most difficult to track.

Two other indicators of input were considered by the committee: public attitudes toward science and mathematics education and funding for education. Examining the results of 15 years of polling by the Gallup Organization on the public's attitudes toward education yields consistent results: mathematics ranks high in importance as a school subject and science generally ranks in the middle. Since these public attitudes appear to have changed little over the last 15 years, and since the relationship between public attitudes and schooling outcomes is tenuous, at best, the committee decided not to recommend the development of further indicators for this variable.

With regard to funding, it is widely assumed that the quality of schooling is a direct function of the amount per pupil of financial support provided to a school; however, research studies do not consistently yield that conclusion. Major cost factors are teacher salaries, class size, and expenditures for physical plant and facilities; none of these has been demonstrated to relate consistently to student learning. Of course, one might speculate that higher salaries would attract to the teaching profession many highly competent persons who in the past have chosen other, more lucrative, occupations.

Even if research results more clearly supported the hypothesis that increased financing yields better learning in the schools, serious problems would remain in using an index of financial support as an indicator of mathematics and science education. For example, data would need to be collected for salaries of teachers in mathematics and science, rather than for salaries of all teachers. In addition, some adjustment of reported financial data would have to be made to compensate for widely differing costs of services in different regions of the country and even in different communities within a region. For these reasons, the committee decided not to use any financial data as indicators of science and mathematics education at this time. Given interest in the funding of education as well as the mixed research findings, however, financial data should be retained for future consideration as an indicator.

In sum, the committee identified a minimal set of key variables that should be monitored, shown below, as a beginning set of indicators of the condition of precollege science and mathematics education. The rest of the chapter presents the committee's findings, conclusions, and recommendations about that condition using the four selected variables. They are presented in the logical order of inputs, process, and outcome.

Although the committee selected for the development of indicators four aspects of precollege mathematics and science education generally recognized to be essential, due to limitations in the data base, only partial and limited indicators of these aspects can be constructed at this time. The committee has developed recommendations designed to improve the quality of available data and thus to enhance the value of these indicators.

Even at their best, these indicators are not sufficient to provide an adequate portrayal of the state of science and mathematics education in the nation's schools. There

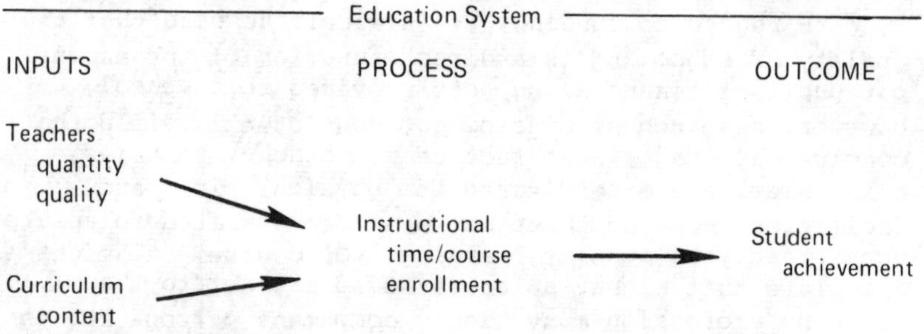

FIGURE 1 Areas of science and mathematics education to be monitored.

is a need to search for more imaginative and less conventional indicators to guide educational policy, including new indicators that have the potential to take account of likely changes in the function and structure of education. Moreover, many important issues about science and mathematics education cannot be understood by numerical indicators. Therefore, any portrayal of these fields must also include studies directed toward understanding the qualitative causes of the observed conditions.

Teachers

Findings: Supply and Demand

Aggregate Quantity

• Forecasts of aggregate supply and demand of secondary school teachers in the physical and biological sciences and in mathematics show shortages over the next several years in mathematics and the physical sciences. A low estimate, based on little change in current trends of overall supply and demand, indicates an annual shortage of 2,800 science teachers, mostly in the physical sciences, and 3,700 mathematics teachers. If teachers currently assigned to mathematics and science classes but not qualified to teach these subjects were to be replaced at a rate of 5 percent per year of all teachers in these fields, the annual shortage would be 9,200 in mathematics and 8,000 in science. Both these forecasts are driven by the education system as presently constituted and do not take into account the possibility of structural reform.

• Aggregate estimates of teacher supply and demand mask great differences among regions of the nation, states, and local school districts within states.

Uncertainties

• All estimates of teacher supply and demand are accompanied by large uncertainties.

With respect to supply, there are three major gaps in knowledge:

(1) The data on the actual numbers of teachers assigned to mathematics and science classes are inadequate, especially as aggregated at the national level.

(2) The number of inactive teachers who return each year to fill vacancies is unknown. Since the number of trained teachers who do not enter teaching or who leave teaching is sizable, this represents a considerable resource. The number of teachers drawn from the inactive pool may increase as desirable job opportunities arise.

(3) The most recent data on the annual supply of newly certified entrants to teaching--3,200 in mathematics and 3,600 in science--are 4 years old. Hence, the effects of current incentives to draw people into the field are unknown. The incentives include loan programs for college students preparing to be teachers, in-service training for out-of-field teachers, and employment of retired scientists and engineers as teachers.

With respect to demand, there are four unknowns:

(1) While enrollments are dropping, vacancies tend to be filled with teachers from other fields who have tenure in a district, rather than with new entrants certified in the field with vacancies. This practice, the extent of which is unknown, reduces the demand for additional teachers, even though it may be detrimental to the quality of science and mathematics teaching.

(2) The extent to which school systems will seek to replace out-of-field teachers or will choose instead to provide in-service training is unknown.

Such choices will in part be influenced by state and federal support policies for teacher education and in part by local board policies and teacher contracts.

(3) To the degree that increased high school graduation requirements will entail having to offer more courses in mathematics and science, teacher shortages will be aggravated, but how much is unknown.

(4) Demand forecasts are generally based on extrapolation of current conditions, taking account of likely changes in enrollment, class size, and curriculum. They do not take into account possible structural changes in the education system.

Findings: Quality

Lack of Information

• Adequate information is lacking on the qualifications of the teachers who are responsible for teaching mathematics and science in high school, middle/junior high school, or elementary school.

• Information on certification, the only proxy available for qualification, is lacking for all but new entrants, although data on a national sample of the teaching force are now being collected.

Requirements for Teaching Mathematics and Science

• Even if available, information on certification is of questionable use as a measure of qualification because state certification requirements and preservice college curricula reflect a wide range of views on what constitutes a qualified or competent teacher in mathematics or science. Moreover, teachers currently certified obtained their certification at different times that may have required different types of preparation; therefore, certification even within the same state does not connote equivalent preparation.

• Although guidelines on teacher preparation developed by professional societies are generally available, they have not been uniformly adopted.

Conclusions and Recommendations

Supply and Demand

- A suitable indicator to assess the sufficiency of secondary school science and mathematics teachers would be either the ratio of or the difference between projected demand and anticipated supply of qualified teachers. The ratio would indicate how close to balance demand and supply are; the difference would indicate the number of teachers that need to be added or that exceed the demand. The construction of such an indicator on teacher demand and supply is at present not feasible at the national level because of the lack of a meaningful common measure of qualification.
- Individual states and localities might construct this type of indicator by using certification as an approximation for qualification or developing alternative criteria for teacher competence. In each case, an adequate determination would entail estimates of both demand and supply under alternative sets of assumptions about anticipated enrollments in mathematics and science classes and new entrants into the teaching of these fields. Aggregation of the state data might provide a useful national picture, especially if, in addition, information was reported concerning differences among states.

Quality

- The disparate views on teacher qualification and the variation in certification standards indicate the need to rethink the initial preparation and continuing training appropriate for teachers with instructional responsibilities in science and mathematics. Guidelines that have been prepared by professional societies need to be considered by the wider educational community, including bodies responsible for the certification of teachers and accreditation of teacher education programs. Requirements should be detailed separately for teachers in elementary school (grades 1 to 5 or 6), middle or junior high school (grades 6 or 7 to 8 or 9), and high school (grades 9 or 10 to 12), with particular attention to requirements that can be translated into effective college curricula and in-service education for teachers.

• The development of guidelines for the preparation and continuing education of teachers would be advanced if the attributes of successful teaching in science or mathematics were better understood. Further research is necessary on the relationships between teacher training and student outcomes; for example, the effects on student achievement of different types of preservice and in-service training and of teaching experience. Current initiatives to augment the pool of science and mathematics teachers should be monitored to assess their effectiveness.

Curriculum Content

Findings

Opportunity to Learn

• Exposure to specific content as conveyed by curriculum materials and explicit teaching is a critical factor in student achievement.

• Although commonly used textbooks and tests introduce a modicum of similarity in the range of topics generally treated within a year's course of instruction, emphasis varies from text to text, class to class, and test to test. Hence, for the nationally normed achievement tests often used at the elementary and middle school levels, there may be a discrepancy between a student's opportunity to learn and the subject matter covered on the test, while at the same time the student may have learned considerably more than the test indicates.

Textbooks and Courses

• To a large extent, the content of instruction is based on the textbook used in a class, yet there is no continuing mechanism to encourage periodic and systematic analysis of the use and content of science and mathematics texts. The Commission on Excellence in Education has called for more widespread consumer information services for purchasers of texts.

• At the secondary school level, and particularly in mathematics, course titles are a questionable indicator of content studied. The current practice of accepting similar course titles as representing exposure to similar material is likely to produce data of questionable quality.

Conclusions and Recommendations

Curriculum Content

• There are no established standards for content derived either from past practice, practice elsewhere, anticipated need, or from theoretical constructs developed, say, from the nature of the discipline being taught or from learning theory. Until some consensus can be reached on instructional content that represents desirable alternatives for given learning goals, it is premature to suggest a specific indicator for this area.

• Although the identification of an indicator for the content of mathematics and science instruction is not feasible at present, this does not alter the importance of this schooling input. Finding out what content students are exposed to is a necessary first step.

• When information on what is currently taught has been collected and analyzed, reviews of the curriculum should be done by scientists, mathematicians, and other experts in the disciplines as well as teachers and educators. The reviews should evaluate material covered at each grade level or by courses, such as first-year algebra or introductory biology; consider relationships among grade levels or courses; and identify the knowledge and skills expected of students at the completion of each grade or course. Such reviews are needed in conjunction with addressing the critical matter of what content should be taught in mathematics and science.

Textbooks and Courses

• At a minimum, periodic surveys should be conducted to determine the relative frequency of use of various mathematics and science textbooks at each grade level in elementary school and for science and mathematics courses in secondary school. Timing of surveys should take into account the common cycles of textbook revision.

• Surveys of textbook use should be followed by content analyses of the more commonly used texts. Analyses should proceed along several different lines: balance between the learning of recorded knowledge (concepts, facts) and its application (process), emphasis given to specific topics, adherence to the logic of a discipline, opportunity and guidance for student discovery of knowledge, and incorporation of learning theory.

• Intensive studies should collect information from teachers and students on topics actually studied within a given grade or course. Observation of samples of individual classrooms can help to document the content of instruction. Such studies could help to inform curriculum decisions by local districts, even though the results may not lend themselves to generalization over a state, let alone over the United States as a whole.

• Improved definitions of secondary school courses, based on their content, should be developed. As a first step, use of a standardized course title list, such as _A Classification of Secondary School Courses_ (Evaluation Technologies, Inc., 1982), should be considered.

Tests

• Critical analysis of standardized tests should continue so as to establish their degree of correspondence to the instructional content of the class subjects for which they are used. Consideration should be given to inviting the judgment of teachers (and older students) concerning the students' opportunity to learn the material that is covered on each test.

Instructional Time and Course Enrollment

Findings

Instructional Time and Student Learning

• The amount of time given to the study of a subject is consistently correlated with student performance as measured by achievement tests, at the elementary school as well as at the secondary school level.

• Time spent on homework is also correlated with student achievement. The attention paid to homework by the teacher affects its contribution to student performance.

Measuring Instructional Time: Elementary School

• For elementary schools, not enough data are available to discern clear trends over the last 20 years with respect to amount of instructional time spent on mathematics and science. On average, about 45 minutes a day are spent on mathematics and 20 minutes on science. Existing information, however, points to great variability from class to class in the amount of time given to instruction in general and to each academic area specifically.

Measuring Instructional Time: High School

• The average high school senior graduating in the early 1980s has taken about 2-3/4 years of mathematics and 2-1/4 years of science during grades 9-12.

• Compared with 20 years ago, average enrollments of high school students in science have declined. While this trend now appears to be reversing, enrollments have not returned to the level of the early 1960s.

• High school enrollments in mathematics have increased over the last decade by about a semester.

• College-bound students are taking more mathematics and physical science courses in secondary school than they did 10 years ago, and the increases were continuous throughout that period. The gap in enrollment between males and females in advanced mathematics courses is narrowing.

• A number of problems attend enrollment data currently available: uncertainties generated by using self-reports, differences in questions and method from survey to survey, and ambiguities created by similar course titles in mathematics that refer to different content or different levels of instruction.

Conclusions and Recommendations: Elementary School

Measures of Instructional Time

• The average amount of time per week spent on mathematics instruction and on science instruction should be measured periodically for samples of elementary schools. This measure would serve as an indicator of length of exposure to pertinent subject matter; values can be compared for different years. Care must be taken, however, to ensure common understandings in collecting measures of time as to what constitutes science or mathematics instruction. Time given to mathematics or science, expressed as a percent of all instructional time, would indicate the priority given to these fields.

• Efficiency of instruction should be assessed by comparing allocated time with instructional time and with time that is actually spent on learning tasks that appear to engage students, as established by observation.

• Time spent on science and mathematics instruction in elementary school should be tracked on a sample basis at the national, state, and local levels. Logs kept by teachers could be used for this purpose, with selective classroom observation employed to check their accuracy.

Improving Methods for Collecting Information

• Time allocated by the teacher to instruction is not equivalent to time actually spent by the student. Classroom observation is needed to differentiate between the two. Time spent on such different components of instruction as laboratory work, lecturing, and review of text or homework may also affect student outcomes. Case studies that document use of instructional time are expensive, but this variable has proven to be a sufficiently potent mediator of learning that the investment appears warranted.

• Experimentation and research should be carried out to develop a proxy measure for time spent on instruction that would permit collecting the pertinent information at reasonable costs.

• Further documentation is needed to establish the variability of time spent on instruction over classes and over calendar time. The results of such documentation should serve to establish the extent and periodicity of data collection needed for this indicator.

Conclusions and Recommendations: Secondary School

Measures of Course Enrollment

• For grades 7 to 12, enrollments in mathematics and science courses at each grade level and cumulatively for the 6 years of secondary school or for the 3 or 4 years of senior high school should be systematically collected and recorded. (See the pertinent recommendation in the above section on curriculum content.) Alternatively, the mean number of years of mathematics or science taken or percentages of students taking 1, 2, or 3 or more years of such courses can be used as a measure.

• The disparities in mathematics and science enrollment among various population groups warrant continued monitoring, so that distributional inequities can be addressed. National data on student enrollments collected in connection with the periodic surveys recommended above may be insufficient for this purpose. States should consider biennial or triannual collection of enrollment data by gender, by ethnicity, and by density of the school population.

Improving Measures of Course Enrollment

• Comparisons of enrollment over time are likely to be of great interest, but high-quality data are needed. Obtaining such data requires consistency in the design of surveys, data collection, and analysis. It also requires reduction of current ambiguities, for example, using a standardized system for describing courses, relying on transcripts or school enrollment logs rather than on student self-reports, and sampling a comparable universe from study to study.

• The periodic studies of high school students have provided useful information, but greater effort should be directed toward reducing methodological dissimilarities. Also, the time between studies sometimes has been too long. Surveys of the type represented by High School and Beyond and NAEP should be repeated no less than every 4 years.

• Time spent on homework in mathematics and science should be documented at all levels of education. Studies need to record how homework is used to support in-class instruction in order to prompt the use of better measures of total learning time in each grade.

Assessing the Effects of Policy Changes

• Many states are increasing requirements for high school graduation; some state university systems are increasing requirements for admission. The effects of these policy changes on student enrollment in high school mathematics and science courses and on the content of these courses should be monitored.

Student Outcomes

Findings

Tests

• It has proved difficult with current test methodology to construct tests that can be used for large numbers of students and yet are adequate for assessing an individual's cognitive processes, for example, the ability to generalize knowledge and apply it to a variety of unfamiliar problems. However, existing tests of mathematics and science of the kind employed by NAEP, HSB, and IEA are sufficiently valid for the purpose of indicating group achievement levels.

Achievement: All Students

• Evidence suggests an erosion over the last 20 years in average achievement test scores for the nation's students in both mathematics and science. Results of the most recent assessments indicate a halt to this decline and, at some grade levels, even a slight increase in scores in mathematics. Much of this generally observed but small increase is due to increasing achievement scores for black students, especially for mathematics in the lower and middle grades.

• Analysis of the most recent NAEP mathematics assessment yields evidence that gains have been made on computational skills but that there is either no improvement or a slight decrease in scores on test items that call for a deeper level of understanding or more complex problem-solving behavior.

• Available information on how well U.S. students perform compared with students in other countries shows U.S. students generally ranking average or lower, with students in most of the industrialized countries performing increasingly better than U.S. students as they move through school. Taking account of different student retention rates in different countries changes this finding somewhat in favor of the United States, but the most recently available data, especially data comparing the United States to Japan, are unfavorable for the United States.

Achievement: College-Bound Students

• There is evidence that college-bound students perform about as well on tests of mathematics and science achievement as they did a decade or two ago.

Conclusions and Recommendations

Assessments of Achievement

• Systematic cross-sectional assessments of general student achievement in science and mathematics, such as the ones carried out through NAEP, should be carried out no less than every 4 years to allow comparisons over relatively short periods of time. The samples on these assessments should continue to be sufficiently large to allow comparisons by ethnic group, gender, region of the country, and type of community (urban, suburban, rural, central city).

• Longitudinal studies such as High School and Beyond are important for following the progress of students through school and later and should be maintained.

• International assessments in mathematics and science education such as those sponsored by IEA need to be carried out at least every 10 years.

Tests

• Developmental work on tests is needed to ensure that they assess student learning considered useful and important. Instruments used for achievement testing should be reviewed from time to time by scientific and professional groups to ensure that they reflect contemporary knowledge deemed to be important for students to learn. Such reviews may lead to periodic changes in test content--an objective that must be reconciled with the goal of being able to compare student achievement over time.

- Work is needed on curriculum-referenced tests that can be used on a wider than local basis, especially for upper-level courses. This work will require careful research on the content of instruction, tests constructed with a common core of items, and alternative sections of tests to match curricular alternatives.
- Assessments should include an evaluation of the depth of a student's understanding of concepts, the ability to address nonroutine problems, and skills in the process of doing mathematics and science. Especially for science, it is desirable that a test involve some hands-on tasks.

2
The Selecton and Interpretation of Indicators

In order to develop effective policy for precollege education in science and mathematics, information is needed on its current condition and on the effects of efforts to improve it. Given, however, that there are limitations to the resources that can be devoted to data collection, what aspects of science and mathematics education is it most important to monitor? And what kind of information is most useful for the lay governing bodies and professionals involved in making decisions about these critical areas of education?

AVAILABLE DATA AND INFORMATION ON EDUCATION

A large supply of statistical data and research information is available on education in general. At the national level, the National Center for Education Statistics (NCES) of the Department of Education has as its main responsibility "to report full and complete statistics on the conditions of education in the United States . . ." (General Education Provisions Act, as amended (20 U.S.C. 1211e-1)). The Center publishes two major compilations annually: The Digest of Education Statistics, issued since 1962, which provides an abstract of statistical information on United States education from prekindergarten through graduate school, and The Condition of Education, issued since 1975, which presents the statistics in charts accompanied by discussion. The NCES and other components of the Department of Education also sponsor periodic surveys, for example, High School and Beyond Study, a study of 1980 high school graduates and 1980 sophomores (National Center for Education Statistics, 1981a), which was extended to 1982 graduates, and the earlier National Longitudinal Study of 1972 high school graduates (National Center for Education Statistics, 1981b). These studies provide information on student enrollment and achievement, although information specific to mathematics and science education is limited. The Department of Education also supports the National Assessment of Educational Progress (NAEP), which since 1969 has provided data on scholastic achievement and student attitudes, one of the few such sources that involve well-designed national samples.

Another source of information is the International Project for the Evaluation of Educational Achievement (IEA) in which the United States has participated. A comparison of mathematics achievement and schooling variables in 12 countries was carried out using data collected in 1964 (Husén, 1967); an assessment of science education involving 14 countries was done in 1970 (Wolf, 1977). New data on mathematics achievement in 24 countries were collected in 1981-1982 and their analysis is in progress; a summary report on findings in the United States is available (Travers, 1984). The science assessment is also being repeated, with 30 countries participating. Both the Department of Education and the National Science Foundation (NSF) as well as private foundations have provided support for these international assessments.

The NSF has special responsibility in the area of science and mathematics education, but most of its data collection activities focus on higher education and scientific and engineering personnel rather than on precollege education. However, NSF does support some of IEA's work and has sponsored special studies on science and mathematics in the schools, most recently a national science assessment using the NAEP framework (Hueftle et al., 1983). Three landmark studies were carried out in 1977-1978 with NSF support: a review of the literature on science and mathematics improvement efforts between 1955-1975 (Helgeson et al., 1978; Suydam and Osborne, 1978); a survey in 1977 of the current status of education in these fields (Weiss, 1978), which will be repeated in 1985; and a series of case studies of schools (Stake and Easley, 1978). Some of the information resulting from these NSF-supported studies and data from other sources have been compiled in a data book (also covering higher education and employment in science and engineering), which was first issued in 1980 and revised in 1982 (National Science Foundation, 1980, 1982a).

Every state also has its own data collection system, much of it devoted to fiscal, demographic, and managerial information, but also including data on enrollments, personnel, and student achievement. There is, however, considerable variation in the types of data collected by states and in the manner of collection, which is not surprising in view of the organizational diversity among the states (and, within each state, among school districts) with respect to their educational practices and institutions (see Tables A2 and A3 in the Appendix). Larger local education agencies also collect information that they find useful for their internal operation as well as data requested by the state agencies. The data from local education agencies exhibit an even greater diversity than do those of the state systems.

In addition to the governmental sources of information, some data are available from private organizations. Educational associations collect relevant data, usually on the supply and demand, pay, and characteristics of teachers (see, for example, Graybeal, 1983). Some scientific societies occasionally survey or study the substance of what is taught in their disciplines at the precollege level and publish their findings.

THE CONCEPT OF INDICATORS

The existence of potentially relevant information does not necessarily make it possible to formulate conclusions about the state of mathematics education or science education--or any other field. For one thing, the data often are not comparable; see, for example, the critique by Gray (1984) of the comparison of state data made by the Department of Education (Bell, 1984). For another, the quality of the data is sometimes too low to permit robust findings. Lastly, due to the massive amount of data, it is difficult to summarize the information or draw implications. The use of suspect data or selective interpretations of data may lead to inappropriate policy, as pointed out by Peterson (1983) and by Stedman and Smith (1983) in their articles on the recent reform proposals for education.

To provide focus to the problem of having to picture complex systems with massive amounts of diverse data, the concept of indicators has emerged. An indicator is a measure that conveys a general impression of the state or nature of the structure or system being examined. While it is not necessarily a precise statement, it gives sufficient indication of a condition concerning the system of interest to be of use in formulating policy. Johnstone (1981) uses the analogy of the litmus test in chemistry, which gives an indication of the acidity or alkalinity of a liquid, but does not provide a precise measure of pH (the concentration of hydrogen ions, the condition that determines acidity or alkalinity). Optimally, an indicator combines information on conceptually related variables, so that the number of indicators needed to describe the system of concern can be kept reasonably small. Limiting the number of indicators is important for two reasons. First, individuals involved in making decisions about such a complex endeavor as education require information that is relevant and easily understood. To achieve the necessary clarity requires reduction and simplification of pertinent information, together with a discussion of the selected indicators that interprets their values and explains their meaning and limitations. Second, since the progress of any field, such as science or mathematics education, can be tracked only if measures are repeated periodically, the feasibility and cost of indicators become critical factors. There are advantages, then, in adopting a small number of indicators, carefully selected to highlight major aspects of education in the areas of interest, so as to encourage continuing data collection.

There are four stages in the development of indicators: identifying the central concepts relevant to the system in question; deciding what measurable variables best represent those concepts; analyzing and combining the data collected on the variables into informative indicators; and presenting the results in succinct and clear form. Regarding the first step, education systems have generally been modeled in terms of inputs, processes, and outputs. A conceptual framework that follows this model but more specifically maps the domain of science education has been proposed by Welch (1983) and is outlined in Table 1.

While the use of such a framework highlights the major areas to be covered, it does not specify the combination of variables that will best portray prevalent conditions in each area. For this purpose, the most important outcomes desired from mathematics and science education must first be specified. Next, the schooling variables that are related to these outcomes and that can be affected by educational policy must be identified. Third, in order

TABLE 1 Domain of Science Education

Context or Antecedent Conditions (Inputs)	Transactions (Processes)	Outcomes (Outputs)
Student characteristics	Student behaviors	Student achievement
Teacher characteristics	Teacher behaviors	Student attitudes
Curriculum materials	Classroom environment	Career choices
		Teacher changes
Public attitudes	External influences	Institutional effects
Goals	. . . etc.	. . . etc.
Advances in science		
School climate		
Home environment		
. . . etc.		

SOURCE: Adapted from Welch (1983).

to assess current conditions and monitor changes, appropriate measures for the identified variables must be selected (or developed). Using these measures and carrying out a variety of analyses will lead to results that can be displayed in the form of statistical indicators portraying the condition of mathematics and science education. The choice of analyses and indicators, like the selection of variables, should be guided by relevance to policy. The next three sections discuss the selection of variables; succeeding chapters discuss how the selected variables might be measured and analyzed.

SELECTING INDICATOR VARIABLES

Outcomes

The outcome most clearly expected of instruction in mathematics and science is the acquisition of knowledge, abilities, and skills in those fields. Some degree of proficiency is deemed essential for all high school graduates so that they can function effectively in society and manage their personal and family lives; additional preparation may be needed to take advantage of further education or to participate successfully in the world of work. The importance given to student achievement as an outcome of education is documented by the many measures developed to assess it, ranging from quizzes constructed by individual teachers to standardized tests with norms based on nationally representative samples of students, from minimum-competency tests that are expected to be passed by all students to tests of material in advanced curricula. Most states have their own student assessment programs (see Table 5, in Chapter 3, and Table A3, in the Appendix), as do many of the larger school districts. As noted above, NAEP was established some 15 years ago to provide information on educational achievement for the country as a whole. Although not nationally representative, the scores made by students from year to year on college entrance tests are frequently interpreted by the media and the public as indicators of academic performance. Public interest has extended to international data on student achievement; the results of the tests administered through the IEA have been used to document the achievement of U.S. students compared with that of students in other countries. Since these various means of assessing student achievement do not always yield consistent results, syntheses and interpretations are necessary; see, for example, the one done for mathematics and science achievement by Jones (1981).

The emphasis and resources invested on assessing student achievement demonstrate the importance attached to this outcome--in fact, the acquisition of knowledge is the main reason for the existence of formal education. Hence, student achievement must be considered as the primary indicator of the condition of science and mathematics education.

A second outcome often stated as a goal of science and mathematics education is the development of favorable attitudes of students toward these fields. Thus, for example, the most recent national science achievement assessment (Hueftle et al., 1983) included items on student attitudes toward science activities and science classes, science teachers, and science careers and about the usefulness of science. It is not clear, however, whether favorable attitudes are to be considered a desired outcome of schooling in and of themselves or whether they are considered important because they are believed to mediate such other desirable outcomes as increased involvement with mathematics and science activities and therefore increased achievement.

Research evidence on the relationship between psychological factors and achievement indicates that classroom morale and encouragement at home correlate rather highly with student achievement (Walberg, 1985), but the correlation between favorable attitudes toward a particular subject and success in learning that subject is fairly low (Welch, 1983; Horn and Walberg, 1984). In an analysis of research results from a number of studies on the relationship between science achievement and science attitude, Willson (1983) also found only a modest correlation of .16 across all grade levels, including college. In the same study, causal ordering results supported the hypothesis that achievement affects attitude rather than the other way around, at least for grades 3 to 8. One problem in the assessment of attitudes and interpretation of results is the lack of adequate theory: as a consequence, some of the instruments and test items that have been used to assess attitudes toward science have given inconsistent and ambiguous results, raising doubt as to what is really being measured (Munby, 1983). Given the uncertainties about the significance of favorable attitudes toward a particular field of study and about some of the measures used, the committee in this report has not treated them as a primary indicator of science and mathematics education.* The committee believes that the question of developing and using an indicator representing student attitudes towards science and mathematics deserves reconsideration in any further work on indicators.

Other outcomes of education generally considered to be important include college attendance, choice of college majors, choice of careers, and later career paths, including life income and job satisfaction. Each of these has received the attention of researchers seeking to assess the benefits of education; each is important to individual and societal goals and to the development of human resources. However, each is mediated by many variables other than those associated with schooling. For example, it has been suggested that plans for college attendance and field of study might be taken as a proxy for student attitudes, but economic conditions and perceptions of future employability strongly affect such plans.

One school variable, additional years of schooling, has been found to be correlated with increases in overall

---

*Wayne W. Welch dissents from this decision.

lifetime income and with job satisfaction, but neither of these outcomes has been tied to instructional variations within the precollege experience, given the same number of years of school completed. (Student achievement, however, does predict years in school.) Despite the lack of strong correlations between school achievement and work performance, employers continue to resort to secondary indicators such as academic degrees achieved and schooling records for applicants without prior experience (Spence, 1973), because degrees and schooling records can be more readily assessed than nonschool variables that might be related to job performance. This use of school variables to select new employees does not imply that career outcomes should be used as an indicator of schooling quality.

In general, the more distant an outcome from the immediate purpose of instruction, the more tenuous the link and the more likely that nonschool variables will affect that outcome. Pending research findings that more clearly link schooling variables to career achievement and other life outcomes, the committee has not chosen to include in this preliminary review indicators representing such outcomes.

Schooling Inputs and Processes

The selection of student achievement as the outcome variable of greatest interest determines to a considerable extent what schooling input and process variables need to be selected, namely, those that seem to have some causal relationship to student achievement. The landmark study by Coleman et al. (1966) and several succeeding studies appeared to throw into question the intuitively obvious connection between differences in schooling and student performance. More recent work, however, has consistently shown significant positive associations between certain schooling variables and cognitive achievement by students. The most robust effects are correlated with "opportunity to learn": that is, whether and for how long students are exposed to particular subject matter. Opportunity to learn in school consists of the instructional time spent on a subject together with the content of that instruction. To a considerable extent, both time and content are controlled by the teacher, although in secondary school students themselves decide at least in part how many units of a subject to study.

School Processes: Instructional Time

Educational practice assumes that exposure to a subject will lead to students' acquiring knowledge and skills pertaining to that subject. Recent evidence supporting this assumption comes from major cross-sectional studies and assessment efforts. One such assessment, an extensive study of elementary school teachers in California, found increases in academic learning time strongly associated with increases in student learning (Fisher et al., 1980). Similar results have also been found for mathematics and science.

Using data from the 1977-1978 NAEP study of student performance in mathematics, Welch et al. (1982) found that, while background variables (such antecedent conditions as home and community environment and previous mathematics learning) accounted for 25 percent of the variance in mathematics achievement, exposure to mathematics courses explained an additional 34 percent. The study was replicated by the authors on three different national samples with similar results. Using another NAEP sample, Horn and Walberg (1984) also obtained a sizable correlation (.62) between the number of mathematics courses taken and student achievement for 17-year-olds. In a somewhat different analysis, using data from a special 1975-1976 NAEP study on mathematics achievement, Jones (1984) found that the average mathematics score of 17-year-olds varied from 47 percent correct for those having taken no algebra or geometry courses in high school to 82 percent correct for those having taken at least 3 years of such courses. While some of the difference may be accounted for by the fact that more proficient students tend to take more mathematics courses, part of the difference remains even after adjusting for initial proficiency (see Wisconsin Center for Education Research, 1984).

The relation between amount of schooling and science achievement is also positive. Welch (1983) has shown a correlation of .35 between achievement and semesters of science. Similarly, Wolf (1977) found a correlation of .28 between science test scores and course exposure.

Based on educational practice and experience and the available research evidence, the committee believes that time given to a subject in elementary school and course enrollment in secondary school ought to be considered key process variables in developing indicators of mathematics and science education. This is not to say that instructional time is the only factor affecting learning or that increases in instructional time will yield equivalent increases in student achievement. Clearly, the quality of instruction as exemplified by such process variables as teacher behaviors, student behaviors, and classroom environment also influence student achievement to a considerable degree. However, given the limited knowledge available about these variables and the constraints inherent in this preliminary review, the committee does not recommend their use as indicators at this time. The process variable of instructional time or course enrollment can be considered a proxy for process variables in general until others can be documented and measured with greater certainty.

Input Variables

Content The content of instruction is obviously another dimension of opportunity to learn. The research that has been done confirms what common sense would predict: emphasis on specific subject matter increases student performance on tests of that subject. Thus, both Husén (1967) and Wolf (1977), summarizing the IEA mathematics and science assessments, report that student test scores in all participating countries are correlated with the teachers' ratings on whether the topics on the tests had been covered in instruction. The correlation of student achievement with number of mathematics courses taken becomes even stronger when the content of the mathematics courses is taken into account: with the variables controlled for one another, Horn and Walberg (1984) found that an index of the number of advanced mathematics courses taken correlated somewhat more highly with mathematics achievement than did just the number of all mathematics courses taken. The common-sense idea that subject matter content, not only amount of time, is important to student learning has been further documented in an analysis of 105 studies on the effects of alternative curricula: Shymansky et al. (1983:387) found that students exposed to new science curricula (i.e., those developed during the school science and mathematics reforms that followed the launching of Sputnik in 1957) "performed better than students in traditional courses in general achievement, analytic skills, and process skills [i.e., the skills stressed in the materials]. . . . On a composite basis, the average student in new science curricula exceeded the performance of 63 percent of the students in traditional science courses."

Teachers The second schooling input deemed critical by the committee is the number and qualifications of teachers with instructional responsibilities in science and mathematics. Classroom teachers are the single most costly resource component in schooling. Although the teacher share of the school dollar has dropped in the last decade--in part because teacher salaries have not kept pace with inflation--those salaries still represented 38 to 44 percent of total direct operating costs for public schools during 1982-1983, even without counting pension payments or fringe benefits (Feistritzer, 1983; Educational Research Service, 1984, personal communication). Moreover, even though the extent of their control over instructional time and content may vary, teachers do determine the nature of classroom instruction.

At the elementary level, the number of teachers is not now an issue, but it may become one as student enrollments increase again in the mid-1980s. Even now, however, the competence of elementary school teachers with respect to mathematics and science is of major concern. Assessing the competence of teachers for grades 7 and 8 poses a special problem. In several states, teachers certified for elementary school are automatically certified to teach those grades as well without the subject-matter preparation usually required of secondary school teachers; yet those are the grades when differentiation of the curriculum into disciplinary courses begins and one would expect the need for greater subject-matter knowledge by teachers than for grades 1 to 6. At the secondary school level, both the quantity and the qualifications of the teachers responsible for teaching mathematics and sciences determines what courses are offered and how well they are taught.

Expenditures and Other Cost Factors In addition to content and the number and qualifications of teachers, other input variables were considered by the committee. One input variable often used to try to explain educational outcomes is the amount of money invested in schools. An effort has been made to determine dollar costs of "adequate" education, state by state (Miner, 1983), that shows wide variability over the states. Differences among communities within states also are bound to be large, and are less tractable from a national perspective.

Some cost factors, especially per-pupil expenditures, teacher salaries, expenditures on books and materials, and acquisition of computers and laboratory equipment have been separately tracked as important inputs. Attempts to relate such expenditures to student achievement have yielded mixed results. In a review of quantitative studies of school effectiveness, Murnane (1980:14) concluded that the primary school resources are teachers and students and that such other inputs as physical facilities and class size "can be seen as secondary resources that affect student learning through their influence on the behavior of teachers and students." Little is known, however, about the ways in which teacher and student behaviors are related to alternative investments, say, in teacher salaries, materials and equipment, school plant, specialist teachers, and the like.

A major cost factor is class size, yet the evidence indicates that marginal (if costly) decreases in class size of two or three students (e.g., from 33 to 30) hardly affect achievement (Glass et al., 1982). In a study of achievement gains in grades 3 to 6, Summers and Wolfe (1977) found that large classes (more than 28 pupils) were detrimental for low-achieving students but were beneficial for high achievers, a finding that might explain the inconsistency of results of research on class size that fails to consider the achievement levels of students. Another major cost factor is that associated with teacher salaries. While salary level might be a good indicator of public attitudes about education, it has not consistently been found to be related to student achievement. Salary levels are related both to the seniority of teachers and to the extent of teachers' education beyond the B.A. level. But neither teacher seniority nor post-baccalaureate education seems to show a simple positive relationship to student learning. Indeed, under some circumstances, a negative relation between student achievement and post-baccalaureate education is reported (e.g., Summers and Wolfe, 1977; Hilton et al., 1984). Since teachers with advanced degrees command higher salaries than those without such degrees, this finding would lead to the expectation that teacher salaries would also relate negatively to student achievement.

In a review of 130 studies that analyzed the relationship between student performance and school expenditures, Hanushek (1981:30) concluded that "higher school expenditures per pupil bear no visible relationship to higher student performance." Walberg and Rasher (1979) conjecture that it may not be total educational expenditure that may make a difference, but highly targeted and selective investments. Yet school budgets, whether local or state, are not constructed nor reported to provide the kind of detail needed to track expenditures for specific subject areas such as science or mathematics. Even if it were feasible--probably at considerable cost--to disaggregate budgets in this manner, the expenditures would still need to be related to student achievement before they could be accepted as a useful indicator. So far, adequate evidence is lacking.

Another approach might be to track federal support. There is evidence that the post-Sputnik federal investment in science and mathematics education helped increase both enrollment and performance in those subjects. But while the programs supporting science and mathematics education within the National Science Foundation and the Department of Education are generally identifiable, some others of considerable magnitude--for example, those sponsored by the Department of Defense and by the National Aeronautics and Space Administration--are not.

In the absence of relevant budgetary information and without further evidence on the relationship between educational spending and student performance, the committee, in this preliminary review, decided not to recommend use of expenditure data as an indicator. Given interest in the funding of education, however, financial data and research on the economics of education should be reexamined in any future consideration of indicators.

<u>Public Attitudes</u> One other indicator of input was considered by the committee: public attitudes toward science and mathematics education. Perception of these fields appears to have discernible effect on the emphasis they receive in school, as witness the current wave of increases in requirements for high school graduation (see Table 5, in Chapter 3). Federal funding may be another indication of public attitudes; for example, the share of the total NSF budget allocated for science education rose to nearly 50 percent in the late 1950s, decreased to about 30 percent in the 1960s, has been 10 percent or less over the last decade, and is now on the rise again (Klein, 1982). But these fluctuations are not mirrored in measures of public opinion. The results of 15 years of polling by the Gallup Organization on attitudes toward

education do not show parallel swings: mathematics has ranked high in importance as a school subject throughout this period; science generally has ranked near the average of school subjects (see, e.g., Gallup, 1981, 1983). Given little change in public attitudes over the last 15 years, at least as demonstrated by this measure, and the uncertainty of the relationship between public attitudes and schooling outcomes, the committee did not use this variable and is not recommending its development as an indicator.

Conclusion

In sum, the committee has identified a minimal set of key schooling variables that should be monitored, shown in Figure 1. Assessing the condition of each of these variables will set the stage for the development of indicators. For example, counting the number of certified mathematics teachers actively teaching in a particular school year provides a datum that could be displayed against other pieces of information: total secondary school enrollment, enrollment in mathematics courses, total number of secondary school teachers, expected demand for mathematics teachers, numbers of mathematics teachers in some previous year, or--if there are separate counts for different geographic entities--comparisons of the density of mathematics teachers related to student population.

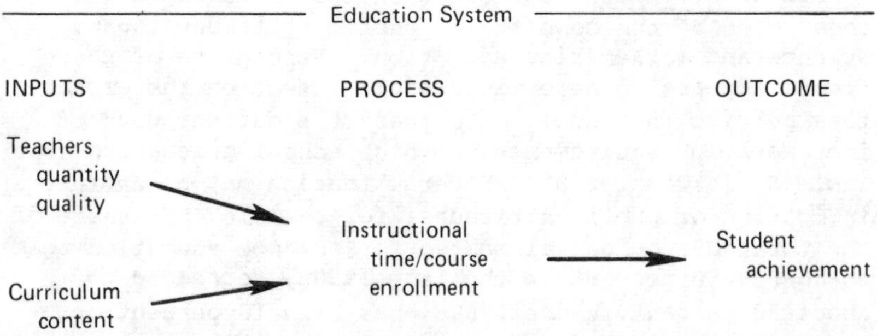

FIGURE 1 Areas of science and mathematics education to be monitored.

COLLECTING INFORMATION

Most of the information available on the variables selected by the committee in the first phase of its work has been collected through surveys and student tests, although occasionally case studies have been employed to describe classroom processes in greater detail (e.g., Stake and Easley, 1978). Some surveys and tests use whole populations, others are based on national (or state) samples, still others are characterized by self-selection of participants, as in the case of the College Board's Scholastic Aptitude Tests (SATs). Some surveys are planned to document conditions at a single point in time (e.g., Weiss, 1978); some, such as several of the NCES data collections, are repeated annually; others--IEA, for example--are repeated at irregular intervals; still others are designed as longitudinal studies that follow a cohort population over a number of years.

Methods for collecting information pertinent to the selected variables depend on the nature of a particular variable and on the types of analyses appropriate for portraying values associated with it. For example, data on the time allocated to each subject in elementary school can be collected through questionnaires to school personnel, but the use of instructional time in the classroom can best be documented by observation. Since this entails time-consuming research procedures, only a limited number of cases can be studied in detail. Case studies are also useful for uncovering problems with data collected through surveys. Thus, data on enrollments in high school courses can be collected from student transcripts, self-reports by students on questionnaires, or reports by school personnel--likely with significant discrepancies among these three sources. Examination of individual course syllabi and observation of the subject matter actually taught under given course titles can clarify such discrepancies. In general, a mix between sample surveys, full population censuses, and case studies seems optimal, with studies linked over time by a consistent set of defined indicators.

Periodic replication of studies is necessary if temporal trends are to be identified, but this does not necessarily mean annual surveys. Careful thought must be given to reducing the response burden entailed in surveys and the disruption that sometimes accompanies case studies. For some purposes, especially for preparing budgets, annual data may be necessary, but for the purpose of documenting changes over time in the state of science and mathematics education, periods between surveys can be 2 or 3 years, or even 10 years, as in the case of the complex IEA studies. One way of limiting both the expense and the disruption and response burden of periodic surveys and case studies may be to set up a carefully selected panel of schools, with systematic rotation of schools into and out of the panel, to provide a consistent data base.

DISAGGREGATING DATA

Collecting Data at the State and Local Levels

Much of the data used to document the several recent reports on education that have given impetus to various reform efforts come from national surveys or nationally administered tests. Such information may be useful for developing federal education policy and for following general national trends. However, education in the United States is decentralized and, despite some tendencies toward conformity, quite diverse in inputs, processes, and outcomes. Each state education system represents a unique combination of factors; so does each local system. The richness and sometimes even the meaning of information is obscured by reporting only national averages. Indeed, nationally aggregated statistics are of limited use in formulating state and local policy: it is states--and localities--that carry the authority for education. Therefore, if the condition of science and mathematics education is to be portrayed so as to inform all the people and policy makers involved in education, indicators must be selected to be useful at the state and local level as well as at the national level. Moreover, the appropriateness of the indicators must be tested against the burden of collecting the requisite information at each level. For these reasons, this report presents data relevant to the selected indicators for several states as well as nationally aggregated data. Each of the states cooperating with the committee already has good data systems in place; the inclusion of information from these states is intended to demonstrate both the feasibility of the committee's suggested indicators and some of the problems to be overcome in obtaining the pertinent data. In addition, even though the included states were not selected on the basis of being representative or exhibiting particular contrasts, the data show considerable variation from the national data as well as from state to state. By analyzing such variations, analogous data on the same indicators that come from different reporting groups greatly add to the value of the information available.

Disaggregating Data by Demographic Descriptors

To serve the national goal of equal educational opportunity, it is important to collect certain data by gender and minority status. The reason for this type of disaggregation is to obtain information on critical distributional issues; for example, different enrollment rates by members of different minority groups in advanced mathematics and science courses may provide at least a partial explanation for different achievement levels. Data for a whole school population (or any age cohort) cannot be used to identify such distributional differences. The underrepresentation in the sciences and mathematics of individuals from some minority groups and of females makes it important to collect data pertinent to input and process indicators in such a way as to illuminate existing differences. Other demographic descriptors may be important for a given indicator. Within a state, for example, the density of population may affect, say, the number of science teachers per number of students in different parts of the state, as may the economic characteristics of different communities.

Separating Data by Educational Level

Since the teaching of science and mathematics in elementary school is not generally provided by specialist teachers and enrollment is not recorded by specific courses, some indicators may have to be represented by different measures at different levels of education. Exposure to science instruction, for example, may be represented in minutes per week in elementary school and by student enrollment in physics, chemistry, biology, and other specific courses in secondary school. Similarly, measures of achievement will need to be different for elementary and for secondary education. A special problem in this regard is the middle or junior high school, which may comprise any 2, 3, or 4 years between grades 5 to 9 and may be considered part of either the elementary or secondary school.

INTERPRETING INDICATORS

An indicator acquires meaning according to the interpretation given to its measured value. There are several bases for interpretation, all using comparisons of some sort. Most commonly, the value of an indicator at a given time is compared with its value at some earlier time. For example, changes over time may be observed in the indicator "the percentage of students graduating from high school who have taken three or more years of science," or in the indicator "the percentage of students who achieve within a given range of scores on comparable tests." Another basis of comparison is among groups or geographic entities: this basis is appropriate to address distributional issues. Thus, it is illuminating to examine the supply in various states of certified teachers of science or mathematics as a proportion of the total number of teachers in each of these states assigned to science or mathematics classes, or the proportion of female students enrolled in high school physics classes compared with the proportion of male students. Changes in observed differences among geographic entities or population groups can, of course, also be related to changes over time. A third basis for comparison is to establish an ideal value for an indicator and record the difference between it and the observed value; for instance, the number of qualified mathematics teachers available might be compared with the supply needed. The problem with this method is that determining the ideal value is usually difficult. For example, a higher demand for teachers might be estimated if it is assumed that higher teacher/pupil ratios are desirable because they yield higher student achievement than if the estimate is based on current teacher/pupil ratios. Establishing ideal values often involves judgments about goals and priorities; it is therefore best left to those making policy about education rather than to those providing information.

For indicators for which ideal values cannot be established, international comparisons (a variation of comparing geographic regions) are sometimes used, as in the case of student achievement. Such comparisons are subject to major methodological criticism because of social, cultural, economic, and political dissimilarities in the purposes and practices of education in different countries. Yet, in the absence of ideal values, student achievement in science and mathematics in other industrialized nations continues to be used as a benchmark against which to assess student achievement in this country. The most responsible of the international studies, including those carried out under the IEA auspices, have collected information on differences in cultural traditions, family variables, forms of educational organization, and schooling processes, so that the ways in which these differences affect student achievement might be examined. Also, the tests used to assess achievement in science and mathematics (as well as in other fields) are carefully standardized. They are based as much as possible on a common core of the various curricula in use in the different countries and thus represent agreement on what students ought to know, even though much of the content of advanced courses may not be included in the tests. Hence, international comparisons of the performance scores on these tests are relatively free of the kinds of cultural bias that would vitiate comparability in other studies less carefully designed and controlled, and the wealth of accompanying information has served to explain some of the differences in results.

All three methods of interpreting indicator values--comparisons over time, comparison among groups or geographic entities, and comparison to an ideal value--are used in this report. These interpretations are accompanied by commentary on their appropriateness and associated difficulties in given instances.

3
Schooling Inputs to Science and Mathematics Education: Teachers and Curriculum Content

Ideally--for clarity and efficiency--each indicator would be represented by a single measure that could be applied to elementary and secondary schools and at each jurisdictional level, the local district, the state, and the national level. The organization of American schools precludes this ideal. For example, differences in specialization of teachers at different grade levels argues for at least two measures regarding teachers, one for elementary schools and one for secondary schools. Because of the reality of the U.S. school system, the committee has not combined various measures into a single indicator for each area to be monitored. When possible, a single best indicator is suggested for each appropriate level of disaggregation. The accompanying discussion deals with the problems attached to the measures associated with each indicator and gives suggestions for future improvements. In addition, the best current values, based on available data, are given for each measure so as to portray the present situation.

TEACHERS

Much of the concern regarding the condition of mathematics and science education has been about the supply of teachers who are qualified to teach mathematics and science courses in grades 9 through 12. A number of surveys have been conducted to assess the extent of the shortage; all of them have been based on the opinions of various education authorities, extrapolating from their perception of current conditions. In 1980, 1981, and 1982, Howe and Gerlovich (1982) surveyed state science supervisors and teacher certification directors on their opinion as to supply and demand for secondary school science and mathematics teachers. Their survey covered 53 jurisdictions: the 50 states, the District of Columbia, Puerto Rico, and American Samoa. They used a 5-point rating scale: 1, surplus; 2, slight surplus; 3, adequacy; 4, shortage; 5, critical shortage. In 1982, 44 of the 47 state authorities responding reported that they saw shortages or critical shortages of mathematics teachers, 45 of 50 saw shortages in physics, and 44 of 50 saw shortages in chemistry. A survey of teacher placement officers (Shymansky and Aldridge, 1982) indicated a decline between 1971 and 1980 of 79 percent of persons who were pursuing teaching degrees in mathematics and a decline of 64 percent of those pursuing teaching degrees in science. (Smaller decreases of 64 percent and 33 percent, respectively, were found by NCES (1983) in an analysis of bachelor's degrees; see Table 3.) A third kind of survey (Shymansky and Aldridge, 1982), of secondary school administrators, revealed that half the science and mathematics teachers newly employed for the 1981-1982 school year were hired on an "emergency" basis, that is, without state certification.

The results of these surveys have been instrumental in drawing public attention to the issue of adequate supply and preparation of teachers in science and mathematics. Numerous initiatives at the national, state, and local levels have been directed toward providing both greater numbers and also better trained teachers for high schools. By fall 1983, 17 states had enacted undergraduate scholarship or loan programs, many of them targeted toward training teachers of science and mathematics (Flakus-Mosqueda, 1983). A number of states are focusing on the retraining of college graduates not now teaching or teaching other subjects. A third approach has been to make teaching more attractive through incentive pay and career ladders. Indeed, according to the Gallup Poll (Gallup, 1983), 50 percent of the people favor differentially higher pay for mathematics and science teachers (35 percent were opposed).

How good are the data being used to formulate such policies? A more recent survey conducted by the Education Commission of the States (Flakus-Mosqueda, 1983) shows 38 rather than 44 states reporting teacher shortages in either mathematics or the physical sciences (physics, chemistry, or earth sciences), with some of the most populous states in the east and midwest not reporting shortages. Has there been an increase in the supply of teachers or a decrease in demand (e.g., fewer students) in the intervening year? Has the definition of shortage changed? Are different criteria being used to determine shortage in different responses, or are there errors in the data? What conclusions can be drawn from existing information? What additional information is needed to formulate effective policy regarding teachers at the national, state, and local levels?

Two sets of questions are paramount. First: Is the number of teachers adequate for the number of mathematics and science courses now being taught in secondary school? Will there be an adequate supply for the number to be taught at some point, say, 5 years, in the future? This set of questions requires a definition of who is to be counted in the available pool, which leads to a second set of questions: Are the teachers at all levels qualified to teach their current assignments in mathematics and science? Are they qualified for the responsibilities they will have in the future? Any response to this set of questions requires defining the term "qualified" at the different grade levels.

These are questions that entail both the setting of norms and the collection of descriptive data before they can be answered: What is the number of teachers available? What is the anticipated demand? How are teachers prepared? How does this preparation compare with existing standards? Are existing standards--for example, state certification--acceptable definitions of "qualified"? The importance of these questions varies according to different dimensions at different grade levels.

At the elementary school level, the question of numbers is not pertinent, since nationwide there appears to be an ample supply of elementary school teachers, at least until the mid-1980s when enrollments are expected to rise again (National Center for Education Statistics, 1982f, 1984a). However, there is concern about the preparation of teachers who are expected to teach mathematics and science in the self-contained classrooms of grades 1 to 6 and sometimes in the block programs of the middle school. For middle and junior high schools, the nature of the questions on numbers and qualification varies according to whether mathematics and various sciences are taught as separate subjects, as in high school, or as part of a core curriculum by a nonspecialist teacher. At the high school level, information is needed both as to the number of teachers and as to their qualifications. But the numbers are dependent on who is to be counted as a science or mathematics teacher and thus become confounded with questions on preparation and qualification. In the following section on number of teachers, the status of individuals being counted is defined in each case--for example, "assigned to mathematics or science classes," "degrees earned," "certified"--without judgment as to their qualifications. The problems of defining "qualified" are discussed in the next section.

Number of Teachers

Supply of Teachers

At the elementary school level, only a small number of teachers specialize in mathematics and science, either as specialist teachers or in grades 7 and 8 when these grades are part of the elementary system. In a survey of teacher demand and supply conducted in 1979-1980, the National Center for Education Statistics (1982e) estimated that 1.4 percent of all elementary school teachers (16,400--15,400 full time) were assigned to teach mathematics specifically and 0.7 percent of all elementary school teachers (8,600--nearly all full time) were assigned to teach science. A large proportion of these teachers are probably in the upper grades.

At the secondary school level, there are available two data bases that have been analyzed regarding the number of mathematics and science teachers. The first is the survey of teacher demand and supply conducted in 1979-1980 by the National Center for Education Statistics (1982e), which yielded responses from administrators of 1,273 of a sample of 1,448 school systems (an 88 percent response rate). Based on this sample, NCES estimated that, during 1979-1980 in public secondary schools, 115,000 persons were assigned to teach mathematics either full or part time, and 104,700 persons were assigned to teach science courses either full or part time (see Table 2). This represented 11.4 percent and 10.4 percent of all secondary school teachers, respectively. At this time, there is no readily available information on the preparation or certification of these teachers. To fill this gap, at least partly, NCES plans a 1985 survey of a national sample of teachers in ten broadly defined fields on their training and background; there will also be questions on how teachers spend their time, assignment of homework,

TABLE 2 Secondary School Teachers Assigned to Mathematics and Science Classes in Public Schools in 1979-1980

Field of Assignment	Total[a]	Full Time
Mathematics	115,000	112,900
Science	104,700	101,000
Biology	25,000	24,300
Chemistry	11,400	10,500
Physics	6,700	5,700
General science	59,600	58,600
Other sciences	2,000	1,900

[a]Teachers assigned to more than one field were counted in the field in which they spent most of their time.

SOURCE: National Center for Education Statistics (1982e).

and availability of resources including teacher aids. Between 8,000 and 10,000 teachers in more than 2,000 public schools are expected to participate; both teachers and principals in the schools will be asked to respond. Information on the preparation of teachers in private schools, derived from a special NCES study of private education, will become available early in 1985.

The second data base regarding the number of science and mathematics teachers is derived from a survey by the National Science Teachers Association (NSTA) conducted in the fall of 1982. Using a sample of 2,236 schools that offered high school curricula, NSTA asked principals how many classes in mathematics or science were being taught and how many teachers were teaching these classes. On the basis of the first 846 responses (a 38 percent response rate), the numbers of such teachers were estimated. Despite the low response rate and methodological differences in the way the estimates were made, the NSTA estimate of the number of persons teaching mathematics in secondary school is reasonably close to that derived from the NCES survey: 106,190 (Pelavin and Reisner, 1984), compared with the NCES estimate of 115,000. Part of the difference might be explained by falling high school enrollments in the 3 years between the two surveys. Estimates for specific science fields are more difficult to reconcile. For example, NCES estimates 10,500 full-time teachers in chemistry and 5,700 in physics; estimates for full-time equivalent teachers derived from the NSTA data are 13,620 and 6,900, respectively.

A third data base currently being analyzed is the NSTA list of science, mathematics, and social science teachers for grades 7 to 12, maintained by grade level, by state, and by subject taught. The list was updated in November 1983, with principals of more than 23,000 schools responding (a response rate of better than 80 percent). Preliminary analyses indicate that there are some 75,600 people teaching biology, chemistry, physics, or a combination of these subjects in grades 7 to 12. Over 50 percent teach biology only, 15 percent teach chemistry only, 11 percent teach physics only, and the rest teach some combination of these subjects. It should be pointed out that the numbers include all people listed by their principals as teaching in the designated fields, rather than only those teaching the subject(s) full time (or full-time equivalents).

The discrepancies in definitions and resulting numbers exhibited in these three surveys illustrate some of the problems with the current data. And lack of information on how many of the persons counted in any of the compilations are actually certified or otherwise qualified to teach science and mathematics raises additional uncertainties about the estimated numbers.

Whatever the uncertainties, the current number of teachers, while an important statistic, becomes meaningful as an indicator only when compared with the number needed. But if estimates of numbers now teaching are attended by some ambiguity, estimates of future supply and demand are even more so. Estimates of future supply must take into account, in addition to the existing pool, the number of teachers leaving and entering the field. Estimates of demand must take into account current vacancies, the desirability of replacing those teachers who lack minimum qualifications for their teaching assignments, changes in total student enrollment, and changes in percentage of the total number of enrolled students who take specific science or mathematics courses.

The teacher turnover rate (i.e., teachers leaving the profession) has been estimated at 6 percent for the last decade (Froomkin, 1974; National Center for Education Statistics, 1978, 1982b). In an unpublished analysis of the survey of principals and a separate teacher survey, NSTA estimates the rate to be 5 percent for science and mathematics teachers in 1981-1982. Pelavin and Reisner (1984), in an analysis of the availability of teachers, use a 6 percent turnover rate and an estimate of 110,000 mathematics teachers and 103,500 science teachers for 1982-1983, reconciling the NCES and NSTA estimates. Thus, they project a loss of 6,600 mathematics teachers and 6,200 science teachers (800 in chemistry, 500 in physics, and 4,900 in other science areas) in 1983-1984. (A 5 percent turnover rate would mean a loss of 5,500 mathematics teachers and 5,100 science teachers.) There is evidence that the teacher pool is aging (National Center for Education Statistics 1983; Feistritzer, 1983), which may mean a higher turnover rate a decade from now due to retirements--at a time when high school enrollment will be increasing and the cohort of young adults that might furnish new teachers will be decreasing.

The supply of teachers can be increased either by persons newly entering the field or by persons returning to mathematics or science teaching. No national data are available on this second component, although one state reports that 65 percent of vacancies in all fields in 1982-1983 were filled by returning teachers (Flakus-Mosqueda, 1983). The potential pool is considerable. According to Graybeal (1983), as of fall 1981, about 6.1 million people (aged 21 to 65) had been certified as public school teachers: of this total, only about 2.2 million were teaching in 1980-1981; 1.9 million had left teaching; 1.9 million had not entered the profession; and 140,000 were newly qualified.

With respect to new entrants, the number prepared to teach mathematics or any of the sciences, particularly the physical sciences, has been decreasing over the past decade. Data from NCES show that the decline in the number of college students majoring in science or mathematics education has taken place in the context of a general decline of teaching degrees conferred over the last decade (with the exception of degrees in special education); see Table 3. (The discrepancy between NCES data and the data from the NSTA survey of teacher placement officers cited above may be due to problems with the response rate on the NSTA survey and to somewhat differently worded questions on this survey and the NCES survey.) It should be noted, however, that neither the NSTA data nor Table 3 include newly certified entrants who obtained bachelor's degrees in fields other than mathematics education or science education, including degrees in mathematics or a science. For example, as

TABLE 3 Bachelor's Degrees Conferred in Selected Areas of Education, by Level and Speciality: 1971-1981

Field of Bachelor's Degree	1970-1971	1980-1981	Percent Change
Education, total	176,614	108,309	-38.7
Elementary education, general	90,432	38,524	-57.4
Special education, all specialties	8,360	13,950	66.9
Art education	5,661	2,392	-57.7
Music education	7,264	5,332	-26.6
Mathematics education	2,217	798	-64.0
Science education	891	597	-33.0
Physical education	24,732	19,095	-22.8
Business, commerce, and distributive education	8,550	3,405	-60.2
Industrial arts, vocational and technical education	7,071	5,772	-18.4
Home economics education	6,449	1,767	-72.6

NOTE: Numbers do not include individuals certified to teach a subject but graduating with a different type of major.

SOURCE: National Center for Education Statistics (1983:188).

shown in Table 4, there were 3,150 newly certified entrants in mathematics and about 3,600 in the sciences who graduated in 1980. These entrants could replace half or more of the teachers lost through teacher turnover, although in the sciences the distribution of incoming teachers is likely to be skewed, with proportionally more being added in the biological than in the physical sciences.

Table 4 indicates the modest proportion of new teachers in science and mathematics who are reported to be certified or eligible to be certified in the field in which they are teaching, 45 percent and 42 percent, respectively. These data suggest that many newly graduated high school teachers who are not prepared in science or mathematics nevertheless may be assigned to teach these subjects. Current initiatives to encourage entry into the field may increase the proportion of adequately prepared entering teachers and reverse earlier forecasts of continuing declines of individuals available to teach mathematics or science.

Demand for Teachers

On the demand side, the National Center for Education Statistics (1982e) survey on teachers also included data on vacancies as of fall 1979: there were estimated to be 900 unfilled teaching positions in mathematics and 900 in science, including 400 in chemistry and 200 in physics. The vacancies for mathematics and science as a whole represented less than 1 percent of the total number of persons now teaching in those fields. However, that percentage does not take into account the number of teachers already in the system who were assigned to classes they were not qualified to teach. Particularly in times of shrinking enrollments, it is not unusual to fill a vacancy in a shortage area with a tenured teacher from an area with a teacher surplus. Fourteen states have no rules prohibiting out-of-field teaching.

Total high school enrollment (grades 9-12) is a major determinant of teacher demand. The National Center for Education Statistics (1984a) projects enrollment at 13.7 million in 1985, down from 14.7 million in 1980, and at 12.1 million in 1990--a decrease of more than 17 percent over 10 years. The National Center for Education Statistics (1984a) also estimates a somewhat smaller decline in the total number of teachers in public secondary schools,

TABLE 4 Certification of Newly Graduated Teachers: 1979-1980

Subject or Field Currently Teaching	Number[a]	Certified or Eligible for Certification			
		Percent in Some Field	Percent in Field Currently Teaching	Percent in Field Other Than Currently Teaching	Percent Not Eligible or Don't Know
Total	79,800	93.8	77.9	15.9	6.2
Special education teachers, all	16,700	96.1	77.3	18.8	3.9
"Self-contained class" teachers	26,400	94.8	80.0	14.8	5.2
English language arts	10,200	84.6	50.6	34.0	15.5
Foreign languages and fine arts	11,000	91.6	72.3	19.2	8.4
Biological and physical sciences	7,900	88.3	45.4	43.0	11.7
Mathematics	7,500	85.4	42.0	43.4	14.6
Health and physical education	10,600	93.6	68.5	25.0	6.4
Social sciences/social studies	6,600	90.5	63.3	27.2	9.5

[a]1979-1980 bachelor's degree recipients teaching elementary or secondary school full time in May 1981.

SOURCE: National Center for Education Statistics (1983:206).

about 10 percent over the same decade. A relatively larger decrease already took place between 1980 and 1982, when the number of secondary school teachers declined from 1,074,000 to 1,039,000. If that rate were to continue until 1990, the 10-year loss would be more than 15 percent. On the assumption that NCES's estimate of a 10 percent decrease over 10 years is more nearly correct, a decrease of some 72,000 teachers for 1982-1990 can be expected, for a total 1980-1990 decrease of 107,000. After 1990, however, there is expected to be an increase of teachers, as high school enrollments begin to increase again starting in 1991. If mathematics and science teachers were to continue to represent, respectively, 11 percent and 10 percent of the high school teaching force, the total number of teachers needed for mathematics would decrease by 7,700 by 1990 in comparison with the number needed in 1982, and the total number of teachers needed for science would decrease by 7,000.

A countervailing factor to decreasing enrollments is the increase in high school graduation requirements already mandated by some states and being considered by others (see Table 5). It should be noted that these increased requirements would not affect all students: in 1982, about 46 percent of high school graduates had taken 3 years or more of mathematics in grades 9-12; 30 percent had taken 3 years or more of science (National Center for Education Statistics 1984b). However, where recent state or local mandates would require more courses than were actually taken before the new requirements, additional mathematics and science teachers would be needed.

A number of state university systems also have recently increased entrance requirements, often beyond those required for high school graduation (U.S. Department of Education, 1984). The National Commission on Excellence in Education (1983) recommended that all students be required to take 3 years of mathematics, 3 years of science, and 1/2 year of computer science for high school graduation. If these recommendations were to be implemented, it would certainly require a large increase in the number of mathematics and science teachers. In the committee's estimates of annual demand for the next few years (see below), it is assumed that decreased demand due to lower high school enrollments will be balanced by increased demand due to higher graduation requirements. However, Pelavin and Reisner (1984) estimate the increased demand to be 8,600 mathematics teachers and 6,500 science teachers.

It has been argued that demand projections should take account of the need to replace teachers of science and mathematics who have been assigned to teach those subjects without the requisite qualifications. At present, fewer than half of new entries into these fields appear to be qualified (see Table 4), and unless countermeasures are taken, erosion of the competence of the existing teaching pool will continue. Countermeasures could include increasing the numbers of qualified new entrants (or reentrants), in-service education, and replacement of unqualified teachers. As to the last, likely replacement rates are difficult to estimate, since the feasibility of replacing teachers, especially if tenured, depends on conditions within individual school systems. Many local systems and states may choose to retrain rather than replace underqualified teachers.

For the purpose of projecting demand, the committee considered three alternative replacement rates per year: a no-replacement rate of 0 percent; a moderate replacement rate of 2.5 percent of the current pool of mathematics and science teachers; and a high replacement rate of 5 percent. The alternative estimates of annual demand, supply, and shortage of high school mathematics and science teachers for the next few years under these conditions are shown in Table 6.

As can be seen, annual shortages are at least 3,700 for mathematics teachers and 2,800 for science teachers; that is, the annual demand for new or returning high school teachers of mathematics and science is projected to be at least twice the expected supply. If school systems were to make a concerted effort to replace unqualified teachers, the need would be for three or four times the expected supply of new (or returning) teachers. Among the various sciences, data show that shortages will continue to be most acute in physics but also prevalent in chemistry and the earth sciences; few shortages in biology are projected.

The preceding summary of the data indicates the considerable uncertainties attached to all the estimates. Moreover, the projections are based on the assumption that the education system will continue to operate essentially as it does at present; the possible effects of structural changes that might be brought about by the application of information technology to education and by other reform efforts are not taken into account.

As noted in Chapter 2, national projections are not very useful for state and local planning. As the

TABLE 5 Minimum High School Graduation Requirements in Mathematics and Science, as of August 1984

State	Years of Instruction		Total Credits[a] Required	Requirements Increased Since 1980		Statewide Mandate for Testing[b]
	Mathematics	Science		Mathematics	Science	
Alabama	2	1	20	X	+	X
Alaska	2	2	21	X	X	X
Arizona	2	2	20	X	X	X
Arkansas	2-3 (5 total)	2-3	20	X	X	X
California	2	2	13	X	X	X
Colorado	Local determination				X	
Connecticut	3	2	20	X	X	X
Delaware	2	2	19	X	X	X
D.C.	2	2	20.5	X	X	X
Florida	3	3	24	X	X	X
Georgia	2	2	21	X	X	X
Hawaii	2	2	20			X
Idaho	2	2	20	X	X	X
Illinois	2	1	16	X	X	X
Indiana	2	2	19.5	X	X	X

Iowa						
Kansas	2	2	20	X	X	X
Kentucky	3	2	20	X	X	X
Louisiana[c]	3	3	23	X	X	X
Maine	Local determination		16			X
Maryland	2	2	20	+	+	X
Massachusetts	Local determination					
Michigan	Local determination					X
Minnesota	1	1	20	X	X	X
Mississippi	1	1	16	X	X	X
Missouri	2	2	22	X	X	X
Montana	2	1	20			X
Nebraska	Local determination		20			X
Nevada	2	1	20	X		X
New Hampshire[c]	2	2	19.75	X	X	X
New Jersey	2	1	18.5	+	+	X
New Mexico	2	2	21	X	X	X
New York	1	1	16	+	+	X
N. Carolina	2	2	20	+	+	X
N. Dakota	2	2	17	X		

TABLE 5 Continued

State	Years of Instruction		Total Credits[a] Required	Requirements Increased Since 1980		Statewide Mandate for Testing[b]
	Mathematics	Science		Mathematics	Science	
Ohio	2	1	18	X		
Oklahoma	2	2	20	X	X	
Oregon	2	2	22	X	X	X
Pennsylvania	3	3	21	X	X	X
Rhode Island	1	1	16	+	+	X
S. Carolina	3	2	20	X	X	X
S. Dakota[c]	2	2	20	X	X	
Tennessee	2	2	20	X	X	X
Texas	3	2	21	X	X	X
Utah[c]	2	2	24	X	X	X
Vermont	3	3	15.5	X	X	X
Virginia	2-3 (5 total)	2-3	18	X	X	X
Washington	2	2	16	X	X	X
W. Virginia	2	1	20		+	+
Wisconsin[c]	2	2	13.5	X	X	X
Wyoming	Local determination		18			

CODE: X = requirements increased since 1980.
+ = additional requirements under study.

[a] A credit is defined as a year of instruction. Some of the listed requirements are to be phased in over the next 3 to 5 years.

[b] May include competency-based tests required for high school graduation, testing at selected grade levels, use of standardized tests, or tests developed by the state or districts. Proficiency tests in basic mathematical skills usually are included; tests in science are less frequent (see Table A3, Appendix).

[c] States requiring 0.5-1 year of computer science or computer literacy in addition to mathematics and science requirements. Several more states are evaluating computer literacy requirements.

SOURCE: Adapted from Parrish (1980), Dougherty (1983), U.S. Department of Education (1984), Education Commission of the States (1984), and Council of Chief State School Officers (1984).

TABLE 6 Alternative Estimates of Annual Demand, Supply, and Shortage of High School Mathematics and Science Teachers

	Replacement Assumptions					
	Zero		2.5 Percent--Moderate		5 Percent--High	
	Mathematics	Science	Mathematics	Science	Mathematics	Science
Unfilled positions	900	900	900	900	900	900
Resignations, retirements	6,000	5,500	6,000	5,500	6,000	5,500
Replacements	--	--	2,700	2,600	5,500	5,200
Total need	6,900	6,400	9,600	9,000	12,400	11,600
Less new entrants	3,200	3,600	3,200	3,600	3,200	3,600
Net Shortage	3,700	2,800	6,400	5,400	9,200	8,000

NOTE: The estimates are for the next 3 to 5 years. They do not take into account any possible changes in the function or structure of education. All the estimates assumed that decreased demand for teachers due to lower higher school enrollments will be balanced by increased demand due to higher requirements for high school graduation.

Education Commission of the States survey (Flakus-Mosqueda, 1983) shows, there is considerable variation in teacher supply and demand among the states. Some states are losing students, others are gaining them. Some of the most populous states in the Northeast and Midwest report no teacher shortages in mathematics or science (see Appendix), while other states are reporting critical shortages. The numbers of teachers do not vary in proportion to student enrollment, since there is a set of constraints operating differently on different communities with respect to hiring or firing teachers. Even among districts within a state, supply and demand is likely to vary, depending in part on the sociodemographic characteristics of communities (National Center for Education Statistics, 1982d).

Quality of Teachers

If the objective is to gauge the adequacy of science and mathematics teaching in the schools, then simply providing a count of the number of teachers in front of science and mathematics classes without any assessment as to their quality is not sufficient. There is, however, no measure available for evaluating teacher quality; there is not even a measure for assessing competence, that is, whether a teacher possesses adequate knowledge of what is to be taught and knows how to teach it. Certification has been used as a first-order approximation of competence, but, as shown in Table 7, certification standards vary so greatly from state to state that certification becomes problematic as a measure of competence at the national level. Certification requirements range from a degree from any of the accredited teacher education programs in the state (which may themselves vary quite widely) to a number of college credit hours in education courses and in areas of specialization. Even requiring a given number of credit hours can result in quite different levels of preparation, however, depending on the content of courses taken.

In the 1960s and 1970s, various professional groups such as the Mathematical Association of America (Committee on the Undergraduate Program in Mathematics, 1961a, 1961b) and the American Association for the Advancement of Science (1970), in conjunction with the National Association of State Directors of Teacher Education and Certification, developed and published standards for the

TABLE 7 Teacher Certification Requirements

State	Elementary[a] Math	Elementary[a] Science	Secondary[b] Math	Secondary[b] Science	Test
Alabama	12 combined		12 combined		S
Alaska	U	U	U	U	
Arizona	12-30	12-30	30	30	S
Arkansas	6	9	21	24	NTE
California	U	U	U	U	S/NTE
Colorado	U	U	U	U	S
Connecticut	6	R	30	30	S
Delaware	U	U	30	39-45	S
D.C.	9	6	30	30	
Florida	6-12 combined		21	20	S
Georgia	U	U	45 qh	40-75 qh	S
Hawaii	U	U	major	major	
Idaho	6	8	20-45	20-45	
Illinois	5	7	24-32	24-32	
Indiana	R	R	24-52	24-52	
Iowa	U	R	30	30	
Kansas	12 combined		18	24	
Kentucky	12 combined		48	48	
Louisiana	6	6	20	20-32	S/NTE
Maine	U	U	18-50	18-50	
Maryland	6	12	24	36	
Massachusetts	U	U	36	36	
Michigan	U	U	30	30	
Minnesota	U	U	major	major	
Mississippi	15 combined		12 combined		NTE
Missouri	5	5	30	30	
Montana	U	U	20-40	20-40	
Nebraska	U	U	U	U	
Nevada	U	U	16-36	16-36	
New Hampshire	U	U	U	U	
New Jersey	R	R	24-30	24-30	
New Mexico	R	R	24-54	24-54	S/NTE
New York	R	R	24	36	NTE
N. Carolina	U	R	major	major	NTE
N. Dakota	U	R	U	U	
Ohio	6	8	20	20-60	
Oklahoma	R	R	28	36	S
Oregon	12	U	21-42	45	
Pennsylvania	U	U	U	U	
Rhode Island	U	U	18	18	
S. Carolina	U	12	12-60	12-60	S/NTE
S. Dakota	2	4	major	major	
Tennessee	3 qh	12 qh	27 qh	24-48 qh	
Texas	U	U	U	U	NTE
Utah	U	U	16-46	16-46	S

TABLE 7 Continued

State	Elementary[a] Math	Elementary[a] Science	Secondary[b] Math	Secondary[b] Science	Test
Vermont	U	U	U	U	
Virginia	6	6	16-27	24	NTE
Washington	U	U	U	U	
W. Virginia	U	U	U	U	S
Wisconsin	U	U	22-34	22-34	
Wyoming	R	R	R	R	

CODE:

U = credits in mathematics and/or science may be required for certification; these subjects, however, are not specifically mentioned.

R = credits in mathematics and/or science are required for certification; number of credits required is not indicated

S = state-constructed test

NTE = National Teacher Examination

qh = quarter hour

NOTE: Unless otherwise noted, requirements are given in college semester hours required in mathematics and science for state certification for elementary school teachers and to teach mathematics or science in secondary school.

[a]Certification to teach; requirements given are for the lowest-level certificate. Many states require additional credit hours for certification as a specialist teacher in mathematics or science or for teaching in junior high school.
[b]Certification to teach mathematics or science. A wide spread in credit hours (e.g., 18-50 for Maine) generally means that the higher number includes courses in several sciences for certification to teach in all of them.

SOURCE: Adapted from Woellner (1983) and Flakus-Mosqueda (1983).

preparation of elementary and secondary school teachers in mathematics and science. The guidelines have been updated periodically (see, e.g., American Chemical Society, 1977). These activities led to an increase in several states in the number of credit hours required in the pertinent academic field for certification of secondary school teachers and of hours of mathematics required for elementary school teachers. Revised guidelines for preparation in mathematics for elementary school teachers and for mathematics teachers for grades 7-12 have recently been prepared by the National Council of Teachers of Mathematics (1981a) in association with the Mathematical Association of America (see also Committee on the Undergraduate Program in Mathematics,

1983); the National Science Teachers Association (1983) has published standards for preparation in science for elementary and middle/junior high school teachers and, more recently, for secondary school teachers of science (Ritz, 1984). As in the past, the effect of these guidelines is likely to vary from state to state.

In an effort to help ensure quality, a number of states have added competency-based tests to their certification requirements, as shown in Table 7; at least 15 more states are considering the use of such tests. Several states provide long-term certification; others require periodic recertification based on continuing in-service education. Districts may impose their own standards in addition to those required by the state. Certification standards are changed periodically as new priorities are set for schools, but teachers already certified are generally excluded from having to meet the new standards or can meet them through inservice training. Hence, certification granted at different times may represent different preparation even within the same state.

Elementary School

In many states elementary certification depends mainly on obtaining a college degree and on a specified period of teaching within the state. In some states, such elementary school certification is also valid for teaching grades 7 and 8; certification provisions usually call for a specialist teaching degree requiring more credit hours in the relevant academic field than for grades 1-6 but fewer than for secondary school certification.

Since teachers for grades 1-6 generally major in elementary education, their college preparation in mathematics or science tends to be limited, as indicated by the requirements (or lack thereof) shown in Table 7. According to a recent survey of teacher education programs (Kluender and Egbert, 1983), 40-50 percent of an elementary school teacher's preparation consists of professional education courses; the rest is usually distributed among general liberal arts courses. If science is taken at all in college, it is usually limited to one discipline. Certification may be an even less appropriate indicator of qualification for teaching mathematics and science in elementary school than it is for secondary school teachers. In any case, little information is available regarding the subject-matter expertise of elementary school teachers presently in classrooms.

Secondary School

Certification to teach a particular subject in secondary school may require as few as 18 or as many as 48 college credits in the relevant and related disciplines. Kluender and Egbert (1983) found that the average requirements of teacher preparation programs for secondary school teaching consist of 25-60 percent of courses required in the academic field to be taught, 20 percent in professional education courses, and the rest distributed among general liberal arts courses. In the large state universities, the credits needed for teaching degrees often represent preparation equivalent to that of a major in the academic discipline, but little is known about the types of courses taken by teachers in smaller, less prestigious institutions.

Because of the great range over locale and over time in teacher education programs and certification standards, and because of the device of issuing emergency certificates, documenting the number of teachers actually certified to teach science or mathematics is only a first step toward establishing whether they are qualified. Even so, no national data are currently available on how many teachers now assigned to teach science or mathematics courses are fully certified for their assignments. As noted above, a new NCES sample survey on teachers is planned for 1985 to provide data on the certification status and preparation of secondary school teachers in all fields.

More information is available on certification of new entrants than on certification of teachers already teaching. NSTA surveyed secondary school principals in 1980-1981 and again in 1981-1982 to gather information on their teachers. Table 8 shows the percentage of newly hired science and mathematics teachers who were not certified to teach the courses to which they were assigned, as estimated from the NSTA surveys. This table also gives some indication of the variations among different regions of the country. It is evident that regions losing population, like the northeastern states, are having less difficulty in staffing their schools than are the regions of high growth, like the Pacific states, where a large majority of newly hired teachers in science and mathematics are not certified.

Similar findings come from the periodic NCES surveys of recent college graduates; as noted above, only 42 percent of 1980 bachelor degree recipients teaching

TABLE 8 Percentages of Newly Hired Science and Mathematics Teachers Not Certified in Subject

Census Region	1980-1981	1981-1982
Pacific states	75	84
Mountain states	44	43
West north-central states	26	43
West south-central states	63	63
East north-central states	23	32
East south-central states	43	40
Northeastern states	11	9
Middle Atlantic states	40	46
South Atlantic states	48	50
Nationwide	45	50

SOURCE: Franz et al. (1983).

mathematics and 45 percent teaching science were certified to do so (see Table 4). These percentages are far lower than for other fields, although English teachers also were drawn from out of field in considerable numbers.

Defining Teacher Quality

It bears repeating that certification is only a poor approximation of competence at the secondary school level and even less meaningful at the elementary school level with respect to teaching science and mathematics. At present, however, there is no other standard that might be used to establish how many of the teachers with instructional responsibilities in science and mathematics are qualified to carry out their assignments.

One unresolved problem is the appropriate combination of knowledge of subject matter and of teaching (pedagogy) and how that should vary by level of instruction (Druva and Anderson, 1983). Obviously, teachers must understand the subject matter they are responsible for teaching, although there is evidence that in mathematics, at least, more advanced knowledge by the teacher does not correlate highly with increased student performance (Begle, 1973). Nevertheless, the equivalent of a college major in the relevant discipline(s) is generally thought necessary for secondary school teachers, with the number of credits required for certification specified by many states. Sequence and content of the courses is often left up to individual institutions, and practice reflects disagreement about such matters as the suitability of courses designed for mathematics or science majors as well as the mix of disciplinary and pedagogy courses. Research evidence provides little guidance. The National Longitudinal Study of Mathematical Abilities (NLSMA), for example, included a detailed study of the relationships between teacher background and attitudes and student performance. Concerning teacher preparation, the strongest positively correlated variable was found to be credits in mathematics methods courses, but the positive correlation appeared in only 24 percent of the cases (Begle, 1979). Generally, teachers with graduate credits or advanced degrees are deemed to be more competent and are paid better, yet the evidence on the relationship between graduate work or inservice education and student achievement is equally tenuous (Summers and Wolfe, 1977; Begle, 1979; Shymansky et al., 1983; Druva and Anderson, 1983; Hilton et al., 1984; U.S. General Accounting Office, 1984).

There is even more question about the suitable academic preparation of elementary school teachers, since they are responsible for teaching subject matter from several disciplines. For elementary school teachers in particular, but also for secondary school teachers to some extent, the importance of pedagogy is stressed by those who hold the model of the college lecture to be inadequate for precollege education. Teaching prospective teachers how to teach science or mathematics is deemed as necessary as what science or mathematics to teach. The how appears to be especially important with respect to teaching such higher-order skills as analyzing and solving problems, reasoning from evidence, checking one's procedures, and in-depth understanding (Glaser, 1983). A third element in teacher qualification is experience, rated by skilled classroom observers and school administrators as a key element in the development of competent teachers.

Experts have not settled their differences, with mathematicians and scientists generally arguing for increased training in subject matter, teacher educators for more training in pedagogy, and principals and school superintendents for teaching experience. Almost all the recent reports on education and several national bodies have made suggestions for how to improve teacher education. (For a listing of these suggestions, see National Commission on Excellence in Teacher Education, 1984.) At this time, efforts are going forward to increase the number of people teaching science and mathematics. These "natural experiments" range from training out-of-field teachers by giving them special courses in mathematics or the relevant science to hiring professional scientists and engineers as teachers without requiring the usual education courses or teaching experience. It would be useful to track a selected number of these experiments through a carefully designed research effort in order to help identify the critical attributes of competent science and mathematics teachers.

Findings

Supply and Demand

Aggregate Quantity

• Forecasts of aggregate supply and demand of secondary school teachers in the physical and biological sciences and in mathematics show shortages over the next several years in mathematics and the physical sciences. A low estimate, based on little change in current trends of overall supply and demand, indicates an annual shortage of 2,800 science teachers, mostly in the physical sciences, and 3,700 mathematics teachers. If teachers currently assigned to mathematics and science classes but not qualified to teach these subjects were to be replaced at a rate of 5 percent per year of all teachers in these fields, the annual shortage would be 9,200 in mathematics and 8,000 in science. Both these forecasts are driven by the education system as presently constituted and do not take into account the possibility of structural reform.

• Aggregate estimates of teacher supply and demand mask great differences among regions of the nation, states, and local school districts within states.

Uncertainties

• All estimates of teacher supply and demand are accompanied by large uncertainties.

With respect to supply, there are three major gaps in knowledge:

(1) The data on the actual numbers of teachers assigned to mathematics and science classes are inadequate, especially as aggregated at the national level.

(2) The number of inactive teachers who return each year to fill vacancies is unknown. Since the number of trained teachers who do not enter teaching or who leave teaching is sizable, this represents a considerable resource. The number of teachers drawn from the inactive pool may increase as desirable job opportunities arise.

(3) The most recent data on the annual supply of newly certified entrants to teaching--3,200 in mathematics and 3,600 in science--are 4 years old. Hence, the effects of current incentives to draw people into the field are unknown. The incentives include loan programs for college students preparing to be teachers, in-service training for out-of-field teachers, and employment of retired scientists and engineers as teachers.

With respect to demand, there are four unknowns:

(1) While enrollments are dropping, vacancies tend to be filled with teachers from other fields who have tenure in a district, rather than with new entrants certified in the field with vacancies. This practice, the extent of which is unknown, reduces the demand for additional teachers, even though it may be detrimental to the quality of science and mathematics teaching.

(2) The extent to which school systems will seek to replace out-of-field teachers or will choose instead to provide in-service training is unknown. Such choices will in part be influenced by state and federal support policies for teacher education and in part by local board policies and teacher contracts.

(3) To the degree that increased high school graduation requirements will entail having to offer more courses in mathematics and science, teacher shortages will be aggravated, but how much is unknown.

(4) Demand forecasts are generally based on extrapolation of current conditions, taking account of likely changes in enrollment, class size, and curriculum. They do not take into account possible structural changes in the education system.

Quality

Lack of Information

• Adequate information is lacking on the qualifications of the teachers who are responsible for teaching mathematics and science in high school, middle/junior high school, or elementary school.

• Information on certification, the only proxy available for qualification, is lacking for all but new entrants, although data on a national sample of the teaching force are now being collected.

Requirements for Teaching Mathematics and Science

• Even if available, information on certification is of questionable use as a measure of qualification because state certification requirements and preservice college curricula reflect a wide range of views on what constitutes a qualified or competent teacher in mathematics or science. Moreover, teachers currently certified obtained their certification at different times that may have required different types of preparation; therefore, certification even within the same state does not connote equivalent preparation.

• Although guidelines on teacher preparation developed by professional societies are generally available, they have not been uniformly adopted.

Conclusions and Recommendations

Supply and Demand

• A suitable indicator to assess the sufficiency of secondary school science and mathematics teachers would be either the ratio of or the difference between projected demand and anticipated supply of qualified teachers. The ratio would indicate how close to balance demand and supply are; the difference would indicate the number of teachers that need to be added or that exceed the demand. The construction of such an indicator on teacher demand and supply is at present not feasible at the national level because of the lack of a meaningful common measure of qualification.

• Individual states and localities might construct this type of indicator by using certification as an approximation for qualification or developing alternative criteria for teacher competence. In each case, an adequate determination would entail estimates of both demand and supply under alternative sets of assumptions about anticipated enrollments in mathematics and science classes and new entrants into the teaching of these fields. Aggregation of the state data might provide a useful national picture, especially if, in addition, information was reported concerning differences among states.

Quality

• The disparate views on teacher qualification and the variation in certification standards indicate the need to rethink the initial preparation and continuing training appropriate for teachers with instructional responsibilities in science and mathematics. Guidelines that have been prepared by professional societies need to be considered by the wider educational community, including bodies responsible for the certification of teachers and accreditation of teacher education programs. Requirements should be detailed separately for teachers in elementary school (grades 1 to 5 or 6), middle or junior high school (grades 6 or 7 to 8 or 9), and high school (grades 9 or 10 to 12), with particular attention to requirements that can be translated into effective college curricula and in-service education for teachers.

• The development of guidelines for the preparation and continuing education of teachers would be advanced if the attributes of successful teaching in science or mathematics were better understood. Further research is necessary on the relationships between teacher training and student outcomes; for example, the effects on student achievement of different types of preservice and in-service training and of teaching experience. Current initiatives to augment the pool of science and mathematics teachers should be monitored to assess their effectiveness.

CURRICULUM CONTENT

Opportunity to Learn

Giving students the opportunity to learn subject matter not part of their home or social environment is a primary reason for formal schooling. The opportunity to learn mathematics and science is dependent, in part, on the content of the curriculum. It is also dependent, in part, on the time devoted to each curriculum area--a process variable discussed in the next chapter. These two aspects of instruction are considered separately for analytic purposes, although they are obviously closely related.

The relationship between the emphasis given a topic in the curriculum and student achievement was demonstrated by information collected by the International Project for the Evaluation of Educational Achievement (IEA) in 1970. In conjunction with science achievement tests administered in some 16 countries, IEA asked teachers to rate each item in the test according to the following scale:

1--None of the students has studied the relevant topic;
2--Fewer than 25 percent of the students have studied the relevant topic;
3--Between 25 percent and 75 percent of the students have studied the relevant topic;
4--More than 75 percent of the students have studied the relevant topic;
5--All of the students have studied the relevant topic.

From the rating data, a national opportunity-to-learn score was obtained for each school; the scores were then aggregated to determine an overall rating for each country at each population level. The results show (Wolf, 1977) rank-order correlations between opportunity to learn science and achievement, across countries, of .51, .75, and .36, respectively, for the three populations tested: 10-year-olds (I), 14-year-olds (II), and all students in the terminal year of secondary school (IV). Table 9 exhibits this relationship for the United States. It should be noted that the U.S. ranking for category IV is affected by the fact that, in some European countries,

TABLE 9 United States Rank Order in Opportunity to Learn and Science Achievement for Populations I, II, and IV, 1970

Population	Rank Order of United States[a]		Countries Testing and Rating Opportunity to Learn (Number)
	In Opportunity to Learn	In Science Achievement	
I (10-yr-olds)	1	4	14
II (14-yr-olds)	6	7	16
IV (terminal year)	13	14	16

[a]1 indicates the highest rating, i.e., greatest opportunity to learn or highest achievement.

SOURCE: Wolf (1977:40).

the terminal year of secondary school comes 2 to 3 age years later than in the United States.

A shorter version of the rating scale used in the IEA science assessment was also administered in conjunction with IEA mathematics testing in 1964. Teachers used a three-point rating scale for each topic in the test: 75 percent or more of the students had the opportunity to learn the topic, 25-75 percent had the opportunity, or fewer than 25 percent had the opportunity. Correlations between ratings and scores by countries was .73 for 8th graders; that is, students scored higher marks in countries where teachers rated the tests to be more closely related to the curriculum. Husén (1967:168) concludes that "a considerable amount of the variation between countries in mathematics score can be attributed to the differences between students' opportunities to learn the material which was tested." The IEA's second international mathematics study and the second science study currently under way are collecting similar information on opportunity to learn.

In the United States, local districts determine school curricula, usually within guidelines set by the state. The degree to which guidelines are mandatory varies from state to state. Most states, although not all, specify a minimum number of credit hours for high school graduation, including requirements in such key fields as English, mathematics, and science (see Table 5, above). For most subjects, however, local authorities have considerable discretion as to the content to be covered within the required credit hours and state guidelines. Some populous states, including California, Florida, and Texas, have state textbook adoption boards; however, the lists of texts approved for school use by such bodies usually are comprehensive enough to allow much room for local choice.

The state education authority in New York is unique in its history of involvement with local districts. Examinations (the "Regents") are constructed at the state level, based on specified courses of study for each subject matter field. Although the examinations are voluntary, all high school curricula are required to be based on them. Similar curriculum guidelines became mandatory for grades 7 and 8 in 1984, and there are also some mandatory curriculum requirements for elementary school.

For some disciplines, mathematics in particular, professional societies have recently developed guidelines for the content of the school curriculum (National Council of Supervisors of Mathematics, 1977; National Council of Teachers of Mathematics, 1980, 1981b; Conference Board of the Mathematical Sciences, 1983). Although there may be agreement on principles by professionals, just as in teacher education, that agreement does not necessarily extend to others concerned with education. As a result, textbooks intended for the same grade or course emphasize different topics; some topics may be included in one test and excluded from another; and teachers may stress different subject matter. Such choices are not always based on the recommendations of subject matter experts. The lack of agreement on course content is especially true for the science curriculum and for nontraditional mathematics topics in elementary school, for the life sciences, and for science and technology education for students not taking the traditional precollege sequence. It will be important to monitor the extent to which the recommendations being made by professional groups are translated into texts or teaching methods that are likely to affect student learning.

The Role of Textbooks

Textbooks appear to be central to instruction. While other teaching and learning devices are in use, such as computer-aided instruction, films, and laboratory experiments, their role is decidedly subsidiary. Stake and Easley (1978), in a set of case studies supported by NSF on the state of precollege science education, found that more than 90 percent of all science teachers use a textbook 90-95 percent of the time. This finding has been replicated over and over by classroom observers. Hence, one way of establishing the content of instruction would be to document what textbooks are used, what scientific concepts, factual knowledge, and processes inherent in the discipline are covered in the most commonly used textbooks, how much textbooks intended for the same grade level or course differ from each other, and the emphasis given by the teacher to different topics within a given text.

There have been occasional studies on various aspects of textbook content and textbook use, but information has not been collected systematically over time. There is even less information available on other teaching and learning tools, especially with respect to their role in conveying content. The most comprehensive information on the use of mathematics and science textbooks comes from one of the NSF-supported studies, the 1977 National Survey of Science, Mathematics, and Social Studies Education (Weiss, 1978). According to teacher reports, one-half of all science classes and about two-thirds of all mathematics classes use a single published textbook or program, and about one-third use multiple texts. Only in grades K-3 science instruction was there any noticeable absence of the use of a published textbook or program (37 percent of the classes). Over one-half of the elementary school teachers surveyed used one or another of the most popular five mathematics textbook series; somewhat more diverse choices were reported in science.

The extent to which textbooks published for the same grade and subject actually differ has been open to question and has occasionally been the subject of empirical study. During the era of curriculum reform in the 1960s, texts in mathematics and the sciences were often classified as to whether they emphasized facts ("traditional" texts) or concepts, processes, and learning how to learn ("new" texts) and whether they included such "new" topics as set theory in mathematics or genetics and evolution in biology. The very deliberate differences built into the reform curricula did indeed bring about differences in student performance. According to NLSMA findings, students studying the new mathematics did better on tests of comprehension, application, and analysis; students using conventional texts performed better on computation, though new math students tended to catch up in later grades (Begle and Wilson, 1970). With respect to science, a number of evaluation studies have recently been reviewed to assess the overall effects of the reform curricula;

after examining 111 studies dealing with science curricula, Shymansky et al. (1983:392) conclude:

> Especially interesting . . . are the statistics for general achievement. . . . Much criticism regarding the new science curricula focused on the apparent decline of general science knowledge among students exposed to the new programs. At the height of the new curricular movement (and even today) the prevailing notion was that the process goals of the new science curricula were being achieved at the expense of the content goals--although no comprehensive database existed for either claim. The data . . . show clearly that students exposed to new science curricula achieved 0.43 standard deviations above (exceeding 67% of the control group), or nearly one-half of a grade level better than, their traditional curriculum counterparts on general achievement measures.

Students taking the new courses also gained on their counterparts in analytic thinking, problem solving, creativity, and other higher-order cognitive skills and in process skills relevant to the doing of science.

More recently, analysis of science textbooks has been concerned with the structure and language used to present topics (Robinson, 1981:5-68). A question of particular interest has been the degree to which science learning involves the memorization of unfamiliar technical words. Building on previous work that indicated that some texts required learning thousands of new words, Yager (1983) analyzed 25 frequently used science textbooks. These included two science series for grades 1-6, six texts at the middle/junior high school level, and alternative texts for high school biology, chemistry, and physics. At all levels, Yager found terminology to be a central feature of science texts, with 2,700 to 3,500 special or technical words included in books intended for grades 4-6 and as many as 9,300 in one of the physics texts. Even if only a small percentage of these words are new or entail new definitions, a lot of learning time is spent on vocabulary. To a lesser but still considerable extent, this is true even of the new texts. Concentration on vocabulary may in part be responsible for a large proportion of students reporting that they are bored with science classes--82 percent of 17-year-olds in one study (Hueftle et al., 1983).

While this sort of analysis points to possible similarities among textbooks in learning difficulty, it does not further establish concordance of subject matter coverage. Despite the key role of the textbook in instruction and student learning, there has been little content analysis of texts since the mid-1970s (Walker, 1981). One might hypothesize that the widespread use of standardized tests would lead teachers to emphasize certain common topics, even if texts included other materials. To investigate to what extent different textbooks treat the same topics and the text materials match topics covered on tests, Freeman et al. (1983a) examined four popular 4th-grade mathematics textbooks and five standardized tests. A set of 22 core topics was identified by analyzing all the texts and tests. Approximately 50-60 percent of the more than 4,000 problems in each book focused on 19 of the 22 core topics, showing that there is indeed some agreement among texts on a common core. The match to tests was rather worse, however (Freeman et al., 1983a:504): "Of these 22 topics, only six were emphasized in all textbooks and tests analyzed. Three topics were emphasized in all books but in no tests. Three other topics were covered in all tests, but they received limited attention in the books. The other 10 topics were emphasized in all four books, but they appeared in only some of the tests." The match between topics contained in the texts and in the tests analyzed is shown in Table 10. The authors conclude that (p. 511) "[t]he proportion of topics covered on a standardized test that received more than cursory treatment in a textbook was never more than 50%."

Variations in Topic Emphasis

Though teachers rely heavily on textbooks for instruction, they use them differently. Another investigation by the same research team (Freeman et al., 1983b) showed that student exposure to the content covered by several of the tests included in the study varied to some degree depending on styles of textbook use, even when the textbook was the same. Berliner (1978), using logs of how 21 5th-grade teachers in California allocated their instructional time, found great differences in time spent on common mathematics topics from class to class, as shown in Table 11. While some of these differences may be

TABLE 10 Percentages of Tested Topics Covered in Selected Textbooks

	Textbooks[a]							
	Addison-Wesley		Holt		Houghton Mifflin		Scott, Foresman	
Test[b]	T(148)[c]	T^1(42)[d]	T(242)[c]	T^1(49)[d]	T(167)[c]	T^1) 49)[d]	T(197)[c]	T^1(50)[d]
MAT (38 topics)	63.2	31.6	86.8	50.0	73.7	39.5	73.7	42.1
Stanford (71 topics)	54.1	22.2	73.6	22.2	52.8	20.8	62.5	22.2
Iowa (66 topics)	54.5	25.8	74.2	28.8	72.7	31.8	71.2	25.8
CTBS-I (53 topics)	56.6	32.1	79.2	32.1	64.2	37.7	64.2	35.8
CTBS-II (61 topics)	60.7	27.9	85.2	37.7	59.0	37.7	67.2	34.4

[a]The texts analyzed were the 4th-grade editions for the series: Mathematics in Our World, Addison-Wesley Publishing Co. (1978); Holt School Mathematics, Holt, Rinehart and Winston (1978); Mathematics, Houghton Mifflin Co. (1978); and Mathematics Around Us, Scott, Foresman and Co. (1978).
[b]MAT = Metropolitan Achievement Tests, Elementary Level (Grades 3.5-4.9), 1978; Stanford = Stanford Achievement Test, Intermediate Level (Grades 4.5-5.6), 1973; Iowa = Iowa Test of Basic Skills, Level 10 (Grade 4), 1978; CTBS-1 = Comprehensive Tests of Basic Skills, Level I (Grades 2.5-4.9), 1976; CTBS-II = Comprehensive Tests of Basic Skills, Level II (Grades 4.5-6.9), 1976.
[c]Topics covered by at least one item in the book; numbers in parentheses are the number of topics.
[d]Topics covered by at least 20 items in the book; numbers in parentheses are the number of topics.

SOURCE: Freeman et al. (1983a:509).

TABLE 11 Pupil Time (in minutes) in Content Areas of Mathematics for Four 5th-Grade Classes

Content Area	Classroom A	B	C	D
Computation				
Addition	33	234	95	26
Subtraction	77	205	248	4
Multiplication: basic facts	40	79	89	142
Multiplication: speed tests	34	51	8	24
Multiplication: algorithm	341	910	720	343
Division	243	19	1,548	2,223
Fractions	54	370	495	2,016
Other	0	82	213	0
Concepts/application				
Computational transfer	49	24	160	147
Numerals/place value (whole number)	0	53	29	0
Word problems	58	3	322	15
Geometry: perimeter	0	53	73	0
Geometry: area	0	103	49	0
Geometry: number pairs	90	40	0	0
Geometry: lines or figures	418	126	70	280
Other	174	128	1,411	68

NOTE: Time was logged over an average of 90 days of instruction observed between October to May.

SOURCE: Berliner (1978:21) as cited in Romberg and Carpenter (1985).

related to differences in total time spent on mathematics instruction (compare, for example, classrooms A and D), variation in topic emphasis is evident apart from variations in total time. It may be conjectured that pupils from classrooms C and D performed differently on division problems on tests than did pupils from classrooms A and B.

There may be even greater variation at the secondary level than at the elementary level in the content of instruction as embodied within such common course titles as general mathematics, introductory (first-year) algebra, earth sciences, or introductory biology. Moreover, curriculum supervisors at the state level report that there has been a proliferation of course titles, with few standards as to content. Presumably, logging which textbook is being used would give some indication of the content of a course, if the content of that textbook is known. Since there is considerable variation in textbook use, however, content analysis of commonly used texts would have to be augmented by observation and analysis of instruction within samples of classes; such observations could provide more detailed information on what is actually taught to students enrolled in a given course. If aggregation of course titles, let alone course content, is difficult at the state level, it requires truly heroic assumptions to infer what "years of enrollment" in mathematics or science collected at the national level might mean in terms of the content studied.

Findings

Opportunity to Learn

• Exposure to specific content as conveyed by curriculum materials and explicit teaching is a critical factor in student achievement.

• Although commonly used textbooks and tests introduce a modicum of similarity in the range of topics generally treated within a year's course of instruction, emphasis varies from text to text, class to class, and test to test. Hence, for the nationally normed achievement tests often used at the elementary and middle school levels, there may be a discrepancy between a student's opportunity to learn and the subject matter covered on the test, while at the same time the student may have learned considerably more than the test indicates.

Textbooks and Courses

• To a large extent, the content of instruction is based on the textbook used in a class, yet there is no continuing mechanism to encourage periodic and systematic analysis of the use and content of science and mathematics texts. The Commission on Excellence in Education has called for more widespread consumer information services for purchasers of texts.

• At the secondary school level, and particularly in mathematics, course titles are a questionable indicator of content studied. The current practice of accepting similar course titles as representing exposure to similar material is likely to produce data of questionable quality.

Conclusions and Recommendations

Curriculum Content

• There are no established standards for content derived either from past practice, practice elsewhere, anticipated need, or from theoretical constructs developed, say, from the nature of the discipline being taught or from learning theory. Until some consensus can be reached on instructional content that represents desirable alternatives for given learning goals, it is premature to suggest a specific indicator for this area.

• Although the identification of an indicator for the content of mathematics and science instruction is not feasible at present, this does not alter the importance of this schooling input. Finding out what content students are exposed to is a necessary first step.

• When information on what is currently taught has been collected and analyzed, reviews of the curriculum should be done by scientists, mathematicians, and other experts in the disciplines as well as teachers and educators. The reviews should evaluate material covered at each grade level or by courses, such as first-year algebra or introductory biology; consider relationships among grade levels or courses; and identify the knowledge and skills expected of students at the completion of each grade or course. Such reviews are needed in conjunction wih addressing the critical matter of what content should be taught in mathematics and science.

Textbooks and Courses

• At a minimum, periodic surveys should be conducted to determine the relative frequency of use of various mathematics and science textbooks at each grade level in elementary school and for science and mathematics courses in secondary school. Timing of surveys should take into account the common cycles of textbook revision.

• Surveys of textbook use should be followed by content analyses of the more commonly used texts. Analyses should proceed along several different lines: balance between the learning of recorded knowledge (concepts, facts) and its application (process), emphasis given to specific topics, adherence to the logic of a discipline, opportunity and guidance for student discovery of knowledge, incorporation of learning theory.

• Intensive studies should collect information from teachers and students on topics actually studied within a given grade or course. Observation of samples of individual classrooms can help to document the content of instruction. Such studies could help to inform curriculum decisions by local districts, even though the results may not lend themselves to generalization over a state, let alone over the United States as a whole.

• Improved definitions of secondary school courses, based on their content, should be developed. As a first step, use of a standardized course title list, such as the Classification of Secondary School Courses (Evaluation Technologies, Inc., 1982), should be considered.

Tests

• Critical analysis of standardized tests should continue so as to establish their degree of correspondence to the instructional content of the class subjects for which they are used. Consideration should be given to inviting the judgment of teachers (and older students) concerning the students' opportunity to learn the material that is covered on each test.

4
The Schooling Process: Instructional Time and Course Enrollment

A number of different approaches have been taken to identify the process variables that affect student learning. One approach has focused on effective teaching practices (Rosenshine, 1976), including the capacity of a teacher to plan and make decisions, use appropriate instructional strategies, and manage the classroom. There is some evidence that careful planning, decisiveness, and consistency on the part of a teacher has positive effects on student learning (Emmer et al., 1980; Brophy, 1983), but most of this research has dealt with elementary school, and further documentation is needed. A second approach has been to identify differences in teacher/student interaction and establish the effects, if any, on student learning. The teacher behaviors that are thought to make a difference include frequency of interaction with students, frequency of feedback, small-group versus large-group instruction, and providing for independent work suited to individual student learning style and progress. Here again, research is not sufficiently far advanced to provide unequivocal conclusions (Berliner, 1980; Gage, 1978).

The one process variable that, again and again, has shown to be correlated with student learning is the time devoted to an area of the curriculum, usually expressed in minutes per day at the elementary level and in course enrollment at the secondary level. Borg (1980) summarized the considerable research in this area. While he suggests that further studies are needed to determine how large an effect quantity of schooling has on achievement, he concludes (Borg, 1980:47): "There can hardly be any doubt, however, that a significant effect is present." An important caveat, however, is to distinguish--especially in elementary school--among time allocated for instruction, time actually given to instruction, and time that students are engaged in learning tasks. A mechanical lengthening of allocated time may have little effect on student learning (Levin, 1984) or may even have negative consequences (Rosenshine, 1980).

INSTRUCTIONAL TIME AND STUDENT LEARNING

The effect of time spent on a subject is particularly evident in mathematics instruction. Even such gross measures as years of instruction and hours of homework are correlated with student achievement: Table 12 displays the results of a general mathematics test given to some 28,000 1980 seniors participating in High School and Beyond. Most of the 33 items in this test were on arithmetic, and all but 3 items dealt with mathematics generally taught before 10th grade. Evidence of even more marked effects on achievement of taking advanced mathematics courses comes from the level-1 mathematics test given to 1982 seniors in the High School and Beyond follow-up. This test largely covered arithmetic and 9th-grade algebra; all but two of the 28 items on the test were based on mathematics taught before 10th grade. The effects on achievement persisted even when adjusted for race, sex, socioeconomic status (SES), and 10th-grade scores on the same mathematics test given to the same students when they were sophomores in 1980: Table 13 shows that the average score for students who took the full sequence of high school mathematics courses is nearly a standard deviation higher than that for students who took no mathematics at the level of Algebra 1 or above, even after adjustment for other factors affecting test scores.

Evidence also comes from data summarized in Table 14, derived from a special 1975-1976 NAEP study on mathematics achievement of the nation's 17-year-olds. A mathematics test was constructed from exercises selected from the first NAEP mathematics assessment in 1972-1973 to assess basic skills in computation, elementary algebra and geometry, and logic and measurement. The analyst comments (Jones, 1984:1211):

> The average score for students who reported not having taken Algebra 1, Algebra 2, or geometry is seen to be 47%, whereas the average for students who had taken all three courses is 82% correct for

TABLE 12 Homework, Number of Courses Taken, and Mathematics Performance, 40 Percent Random Sample of High School and Beyond 1980 Seniors

Time on Homework per week	Standard Score (mean 50)	Standard Deviation (10.0)	Completed Courses Grades 10-12 Mathematics	Standard Score (mean 50)	Standard Deviation (10.0)	Advanced Math Courses Taken	Standard Score (mean 50)	Standard Deviation (10.0)
None assigned	45	7.7	none	44	7.4	No math	41	7.1
None done	47	9.4	0.5 yr	43	7.7	Alg. 1	44	7.1
Less than 1 h	49	9.8	1	46	8.2	Alg. 1 + geo.	50	7.3
5-10 h	53	9.7	1.5	48	9.5	Alg. 1 + 2	46	7.3
More than 10 h	57	9.2	2	49	9.4	Alg. 1, 2, geo.	54	7.9
			2.5	51	9.3	All but calc.	59	6.3
			3	55	10.0	All adv. math	63	5.2
			More than 3	56	10.0			

SOURCE: Table prepared for the committee by the Wisconsin Center for Education Research, based on a special analysis of HSB data.

TABLE 13 Effect of Taking Mathematics Courses on Mathematics Achievement, High School and Beyond 1982 Seniors in Public School (Mean Score on Mathematics I Test = 51.3; Standard Deviation = 10)

Mathematics Courses	Deviation Unadjusted	Deviation Adjusted for Race and Sex	Deviation Adjusted for Race, Sex, Previous Mathematics Achievement, and SES
No math	-8.57	-8.10	-3.72
Algebra 1	-4.61	-4.37	-1.94
Algebra 1, 2	-2.31	-2.02	-0.90
Algebra 1, geometry	0.49	0.25	-0.01
Algebra 1, 2, geometry	3.88	3.81	1.94
Algebra 1, 2, geometry, trigonometry	9.14	8.62	4.11
All advanced	13.12	12.32	4.99
Difference between no math and all math	21.69	20.42	8.71

SOURCE: Table prepared for the committee by the Wisconsin Center for Education Research, based on a special analysis of HSB data.

TABLE 14 Average Mathematics Score (Percent Correct) by Number of Years of Algebra 1, Geometry, and Algebra 2 for 17-Year-Olds, 1975-1976

Number of Years of Courses	Average Score	Percent of Students with 0, 1, 2, or 3 Years		
		Black	White	All
0	47	29	18	20
1	59	37	24	26
2	70	21	26	25
3	82	13	32	29

SOURCE: Adapted from Jones (1984:1211).

> the same mathematics exercises. This is a difference of nearly two standard deviations. The relation of mathematics achievement to courses taken is strong and clear. . . . The data . . . show a disproportionate representation of black students and white students for differing numbers of years of high school algebra and geometry. About two thirds of black students but only 42% of white students report having taken 0 or 1 year of high school algebra and geometry. This difference between black and white students in algebra and geometry enrollments might be responsible for a large part of the white-black average difference in mathematics achievement scores.

Jones's conjecture appears to be borne out by the previously cited results of the mathematics test (level 1) taken by the 1982 high school seniors in the High School and Beyond follow-up. The mean test score was 51.6, with a standard deviation of 10 (see Table 13). When scores were adjusted for courses taken, the difference in unadjusted scores between males and females (adjusted for race) was reduced from 1.52 to 1.08; the difference between blacks and Asians (adjusted for sex) dropped from 12.58 to 5.25; and the difference between Asians and whites (adjusted for sex) changed from 4.07 in favor of Asians to 1.26 in favor of whites.

The strong relationship between enrollment in high school mathematics courses and test scores is likely, in part, to result from the choices of high achievers to enroll in more mathematics courses and the choices of low achievers to enroll in fewer courses. In the data from High School and Beyond, however, senior mathematics scores are related to mathematics courses taken, even after adjusting not only for race, sex, and SES, but also for earlier (sophomore) scores on the mathematics test (see final column, Table 13); this strongly suggests that course taking per se influences test performance.

Although testing for science achievement is less common than for mathematics achievement, both Welch (1983) and Wolf (1977) found positive correlations between science test scores and semesters of science or course exposure. The correlations are somewhat lower than in mathematics, possibly because of the less sequential character of the science curriculum.

Given the robust findings regarding this variable and the need to limit the number of indicators, the committee selected instructional time given to a subject to stand as a proxy for schooling processes in general. Even so, measurement of this variable is not simple. The complications include: discrepancies between time scheduled for a subject in school and time actually devoted to instruction; time used for homework; and the different organization of elementary and secondary education, requiring different approaches to measuring time spent on a subject. These issues are discussed below.

Allocated Versus Actual Instructional Time

A recent research review (Karweit, 1983) on the time used for instruction concludes that, at most, instruction in elementary school may occupy 60 percent of the 6-hour school day; this is reduced further by student absences and student inattention. This loss of time from instruction is not a new phenomenon; some 20 years ago, Philip W. Jackson (1965) published a landmark description of life in the classroom that vividly drove home this point. Classroom observation has continued to document the extent to which students are actually engaged in learning during instruction. An example of such observation done on 21 5th-grade classrooms in California is given in Table 15, which shows that students are inattentive for as much as a one-third of instructional time.

With respect to absences, the same study found that, of the 180 days in a school year, 30 days are usually lost to classroom instruction due to field trips, student

TABLE 15 Allocated and Pupil Engaged Time in Mathematics for Four 5th-Grade Classes

Time	Classes A	B	C	D
Number of days data collected	73	89	91	93
Average minutes allocated daily	23	28	61	57
Percent of time students engaged	74	80	80	66
Engaged minutes per day	17	22	49	38

SOURCE: Berliner (1978:21) as cited in Romberg and Carpenter (1985).

illness, a Christmas play, and the like (Berliner et al., 1978), although field trips and some extracurricular activities may enhance learning. At the same time, poor use of instructional time inhibits the effectiveness of teachers. Karweit (1983) points out that, even under the most favorable assumptions of minimal school absence and loss of instructional time, students are occupied with actual learning only a little more than one-half their scheduled time in school; for some students, it may be less than one-third of the time.

While there have been fewer systematic studies of time use in secondary school, anecdotal information gives little reason to think that the situation is much different (see, e.g., Boyer, 1983).

Homework

Homework is an inexpensive way of extending instructional time. In addition to the data from High School and Beyond, evidence on its relationship to student performance also comes from the first IEA mathematics assessment. Husén (1967) reports a strong positive correlation between mean mathematics scores for all countries and mean hours spent on all homework as well as on mathematics homework specifically. According to the IEA findings, a bit more than one-third of all homework time, on average, is spent on mathematics in all countries. These findings, based on student self-reports from the 1964 mathematics assessment, indicate that 8th

TABLE 16 Hours per Week Scheduled for Mathematics: 8th Graders and Mathematics Students in Senior Year (1964 Data)

	Mathematics Instruction				Mathematics Homework			
	8th Grade		Seniors		8th Grade		Seniors	
Country	Mean	SD	Mean	SD	Mean	SD	Mean	SD
Australia	5.2	.6	6.9	1.6	2.5	1.6	6.1	3.3
Belgium	4.7	1.0	7.4	1.1	3.7	2.5	8.7	4.6
England	4.0	.8	4.4	1.3	1.8	.9	4.1	1.9
Finland	3.0	.2	4.0	0	2.9	2.2	6.6	3.5
France	4.4	.8	8.9	.5	3.4	1.9	9.6	3.5
Germany	3.9	.6	4.2	.5	3.4	1.9	5.1	2.a
Netherlands	4.6	1.5	5.1	.3	2.6	1.9	5.7	3.4
Israel	4.1	.5	5.0	.3	4.4	2.6	7.5	3.7
Japan	4.5	.5	5.4	1.1	3.0	1.8	5.2	4.3
Scotland	4.6	1.0	6.2	1.5	2.2	1.6	4.1	2.3
Sweden	3.8	.9	4.6	1.6	1.9	1.3	4.9	2.9
United States	4.6	1.3	5.0	.9	3.1	2.3	4.1	2.4

NOTE: Hours of instruction may refer to periods somewhat shorter than 60 minutes.

SOURCE: Husén (1967, Vol. I:278).

graders in the United States spent about 3.1 hours per week on mathematics homework, slightly above the average for all countries (see Table 16). For mathematics students in the last year of secondary school, however, the required hours of homework in most countries doubled between 8th grade and 12th grade, while in the United States the increase was only from 3 to 4 hours per week. This difference may have contributed to the poorer performance of older U.S. students on the IEA tests. Data on homework were again collected by IEA from students and teachers in 1981-1982 during the Second International Mathematics Study; the teacher responses have been analyzed. For U.S. 8th graders, teachers estimated that the time typically spent on assigned homework was 2.3 hours per week; 75 percent of the students were estimated to spend 3 hours or less. For 12th graders, teachers reported that they expected an average 4 hours of homework per week from students in precalculus classes and 5 hours from students in calculus classes (Travers, 1984).

Most other information available on the amount of homework done by students is not specific as to subject matter. Studies done on high school seniors in 1972 and

1980 show that time spent on all homework dropped during this period: the number of seniors who reported that they spent at least 5 hours per week on homework decreased from 35.2 to 24.5 percent, with decreases greatest in the south (36 to 21 percent) (National Center for Education Statistics, 1984c). The average amount of homework time reported was 3.9 hours per week, down from 4.3 hours in 1972, although the amount of homework effort reported by students in academic programs remained virtually constant at 5.1 hours (National Center for Education Statistics, 1984c). In contrast, according to a recent study (Fetters et al., 1983), six times as many seniors in Japan spend more than 10 hours per week on homework as in America (36 compared with 6 percent) and two-thirds of the Japanese students spend at least 5 hours on homework compared with one-fourth in America.

Research evidence indicates that the way homework assignments are treated affects the contribution of homework to student achievement (Walberg, 1985). Checks on completion, discussion in class, and correction by the teacher greatly increase the value of homework. Hence, attempts to track hours of homework should not only record the subject in which the homework is assigned, but also the way homework is used to support classroom instruction.

MEASURING INSTRUCTIONAL TIME

The organization of high school according to curriculum area permits tracking instructional time through course enrollment, at least as a first approximation. For elementary school, studies have been made of the time spent on specific subjects, documented by classroom observation to determine actual versus allocated instructional time. The method to be used for tracking time for grades 7 and 8 varies depending on their organization.

Elementary School

Recent national data on time scheduled for mathematics in grades 1-6 come from three sources, one of which--the Weiss (1978) survey--also collected information on science instruction. Data reported by teachers, shown in Table 17, indicate that time spent in teaching mathematics and science increases somewhat in the upper elementary grades; average time increases from 41 minutes in grades K-3 to

TABLE 17 Average Number of Minutes Per Day Spent Teaching Each Subject in Self-Contained Classes, by Grade

	Grades					
	K-3		4-6		Total	
Subject	Average Number of Minutes	Standard Error	Average Number of Minutes	Standard Error	Average Number of Minutes	Standard Error
Mathematics	41	.61	51	.43	44	.38
Science	17	.24	28	.64	20	.28
Social Studies	21	.62	34	.71	25	.53
Reading	95	1.60	66	1.34	86	1.18
Sample N	467		302		769	

NOTE: The data are based on teacher self-reports.

SOURCE: Weiss (1978:51).

51 minutes in grades 4-6 for mathematics and from 17 to 28 minutes for science. Collecting information on time spent on science instruction in grades 1-6 is difficult because there is no common understanding on what subjects in elementary school are actually considered part of science. With the coming of more work using computers, mathematics will also become more difficult to define.

The second source of information is the Sustaining Effects Study (Wang et al., 1978), which examined the nature and effectiveness of Title I compensatory education programs. The data from this study show more time spent on mathematics per day than do the Weiss data, ranging from 47 to 68 minutes. One striking finding is a lowered emphasis on reading in the upper grades (see Figure 2). Information from the previously mentioned California study (Berliner et al., 1978) shows the range of time allocated to mathematics in 5th grade to be from 23 to 61 minutes per day (see Table 15, above); about the same amount of variation was observed in 2nd grade. According to these data, students in one classroom spent nearly three times as much time on mathematics as did students in another class of the same grade.

Similar variability has been observed in time allocation studies over the past 60 years. Because several of these studies recorded their methodology with great care, it is possible to compare allocation of instructional time over the last 100 years (Borg, 1980); see Figure 3. It is interesting that the time allocated to mathematics instruction has stayed relatively stable, considering the general decrease in time devoted to all academic instruction.

The amount of time scheduled for mathematics instruction in 8th grade is approximately the same as that in elementary school, according to the 1964 IEA data. Comparison with 11 other industrialized countries shows that the mean hours of mathematics instruction reported for the United States were exceeded only in Australia and Belgium; there was greater variation around the mean in the United States than in most other countries (see Table 16, above). Similar information, including time spent on specific topics, was collected in 1981-1982 during the Second International Mathematics Study. Preliminary results for the United States indicate that, while mathematics is generally taught 5 periods per week in 8th grade, class length can vary from 40 to 60 minutes. Thus, while the median number of clock hours of mathematics instruction per year is 145, the range is from 115 to 180 hours (Travers, 1984).

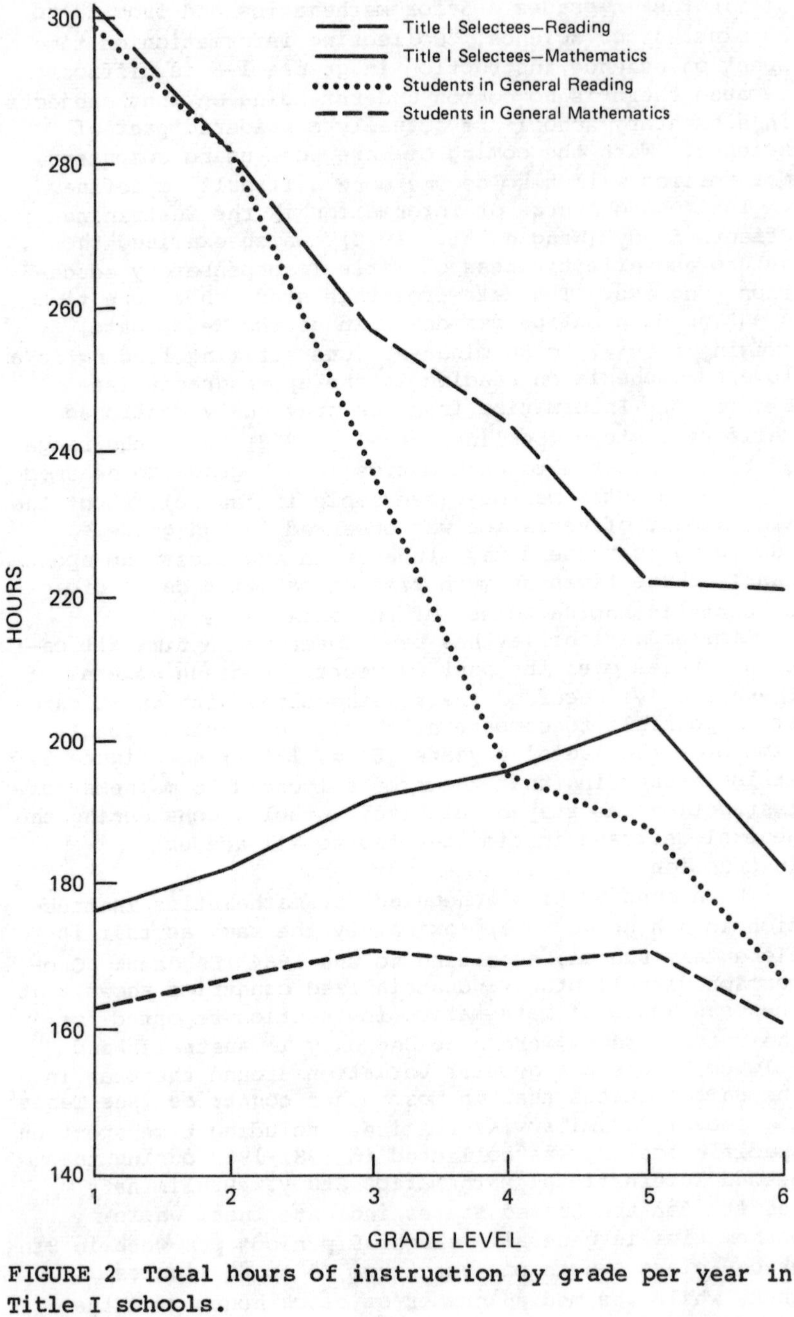

FIGURE 2 Total hours of instruction by grade per year in Title I schools.

SOURCE: Wang et al. (1978:71).

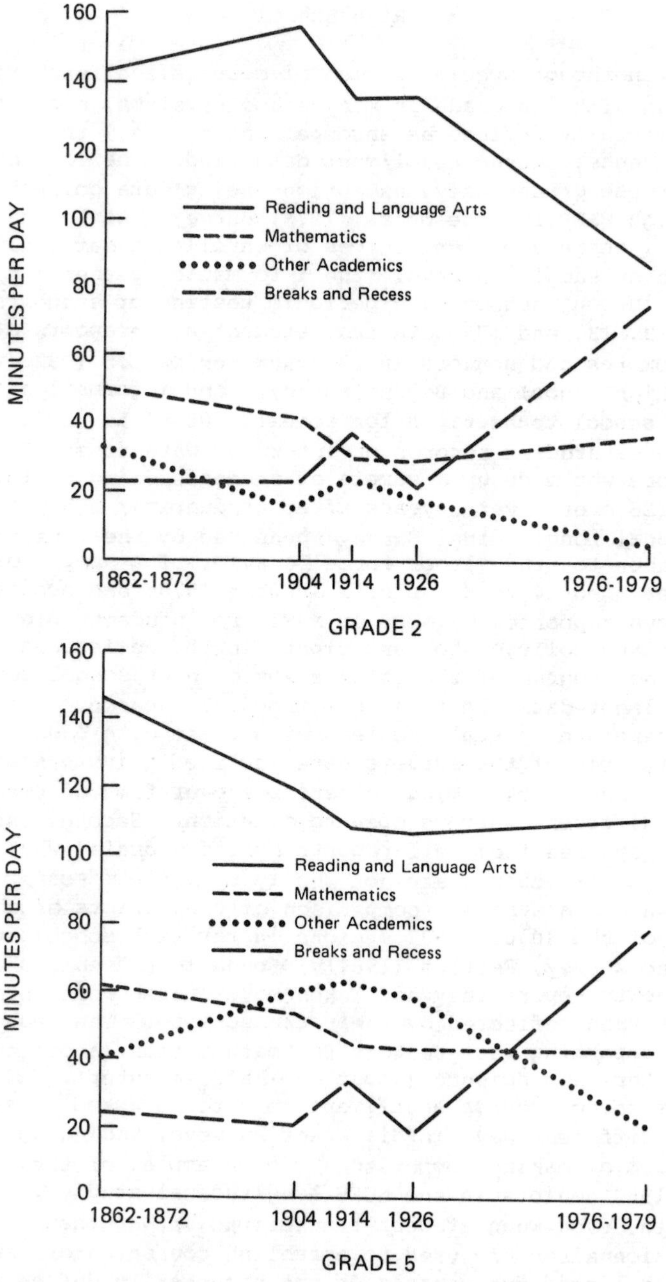

FIGURE 3 Time allocations in minutes per day across the decades.

SOURCE: Borg (1980:44).

High School

Even though specialization of courses and teachers begins with 7th grade in many school systems, high school is generally defined as encompassing grades 9 through 12. Hence, course enrollment data tend to be collected for those grades only, exceptions being data collected through NAEP and the Weiss (1978) survey. At the national level, there are five sources of enrollment data, all based on sample surveys: the information gathered by NAEP in conjunction with periodic testing of students at ages 9, 13, and 17; data from student self-reports of sophomores and seniors in 1980 and seniors in 1982 (from the High School and Beyond surveys) and information from high school transcripts for some 12,000 of the 1982 seniors; student records or interview data from 1972 seniors who made up a sample of students being followed by NCES over several years after graduation; a 5-year National Longitudinal Survey sponsored by the Department of Labor to study labor force behavior of a sample of youths aged 14 to 22 as of 1 January 1979; and occasional surveys supported by NCES or NSF. For students planning to attend college who participate in the Admissions Testing Program of the College Board, high school course enrollment data are available from this source.

There are several problems with these data bases. First, some of the surveys have included private schools, others have not, making comparisons over time of results from different surveys open to question. Second, the data gathered from self-reports by individuals, whether students or others, are not wholly reliable. For instance, in a recent comparison of transcripts of about half of the 30,000 1982 seniors in the High School and Beyond survey, Fetters (1984:v) found that "seniors tended to report they had taken more course work in most areas than reflected by their transcripts. The amount of over-reporting was greatest for mathematics (about one semester) and science (about one-half semester)." Third, questions on course enrollment tend to be asked in somewhat different ways in different surveys, adding to the problem of making comparisons, for example, of the 1972 and 1980 seniors in the NCES longitudinal studies. Fourth, even when student transcripts rather than questionnaires are used to establish course enrollments, titles listed for courses do not necessarily define the content or the level. Not infrequently, there are as many as three "Algebra I" courses offered in the same high school, each at a different level of difficulty. "Algebra II" may mean either the second semester of first-year algebra or the second full year of algebra. Also, course periods may be of different duration, and there may be a different number of periods scheduled for courses with the same label. These differences make the numbers pertaining to semesters or years of a subject studied somewhat ambiguous and difficult to interpret when averaged over a state or reported on national samples.

Enrollment data tend to be reported in three different ways: percentage of seniors who have taken 1, 2, or 3 (or more) years of science or mathematics; percentage of seniors who have taken some specific course; and percentage of the total number of high school students (or of a particular grade) taking a specific course. In part because of the inclusion of grade 9 in some of the data but not in others, the different data sets are not readily reconcilable. It must also be remembered that enrollment data deal only with students still in school, not the total age cohort, many of whom drop out of school before graduation.

The High School and Beyond data (National Center for Education Statistics, 1981a), based on student self-reports, yield information both on total mathematics and science enrollments and on individual college preparatory courses for 1980 seniors. The data for grades 10-12, given in Tables 18 and 19, show total enrollments in various courses and also indicate differences between males and females and among different ethnic groups. Preliminary data for 1982 seniors (Wisconsin Center for

TABLE 18 Cumulative Percentage of 1980 and 1982 High School Seniors Reporting Varying Amounts of Mathematics and Science Coursework Taken, by Sex--Grades 10-12

Amount of Coursework	Mathematics			Sciences		
	All	Male	Female	All	Male	Female
Total, including those with no coursework	100 (100)	100 (100)	100 (100)	100 (100)	100 (100)	100 (100)
1 year or more	93 (93)	94 (93)	92 (93)	90 (89)	91 (89)	89 (89)
2 years or more	67 (68)	71 (70)	63 (66)	53 (53)	57 (56)	50 (50)
3 years or more	34 (35)	40 (39)	28 (31)	23 (22)	27 (25)	19 (19)

NOTE: Preliminary figures for 1982 seniors are shown in parentheses; figures provided by the Wisconsin Center for Education Research (1984).

SOURCE (for 1980 seniors): National Center for Education Statistics (1981a:3).

TABLE 19 Percentage of 1980 and 1982 High School Seniors Reporting Mathematics and Science Courses Taken, by Course Title, and by Sex and Racial/Ethnic Group--Grades 10-12

Course	All seniors	Sex		Racial/Ethnic Group			American Indian or Alaskan Native	Asian or Pacific Islander
		Male	Female	Hispanic	Black	White		
Algebra I	79 (78)	79 (76)	79 (79)	67 (63)	68 (69)	81 (82)	61 (54)	88 (92)
Algebra II	49 (48)	51 (49)	47 (48)	38 (33)	39 (41)	50 (52)	32 (31)	76 (76)
Geometry	56 (55)	58 (55)	55 (55)	39 (34)	38 (41)	60 (60)	34 (31)	79 (81)
Trigonometry	26 (26)	30 (29)	22 (23)	15 (13)	15 (15)	27 (29)	17 (13)	50 (53)
Calculus	8 (9)	10 (10)	6 (8)	4 (4)	5 (3)	8 (10)	5 (4)	22 (25)
Physics	19 (21)	26 (26)	14 (16)	15 (17)	19 (20)	20 (21)	17 (35)	35 (47)
Chemistry	37 (39)	39 (39)	35 (36)	26 (23)	28 (31)	39 (40)	24 (37)	59 (67)

NOTE: Preliminary figures for 1982 seniors are shown in parentheses; figures provided by the Wisconsin Center for Education Research (1984).

SOURCE (for 1980 seniors): National Center for Education Statistics (1981a:5).

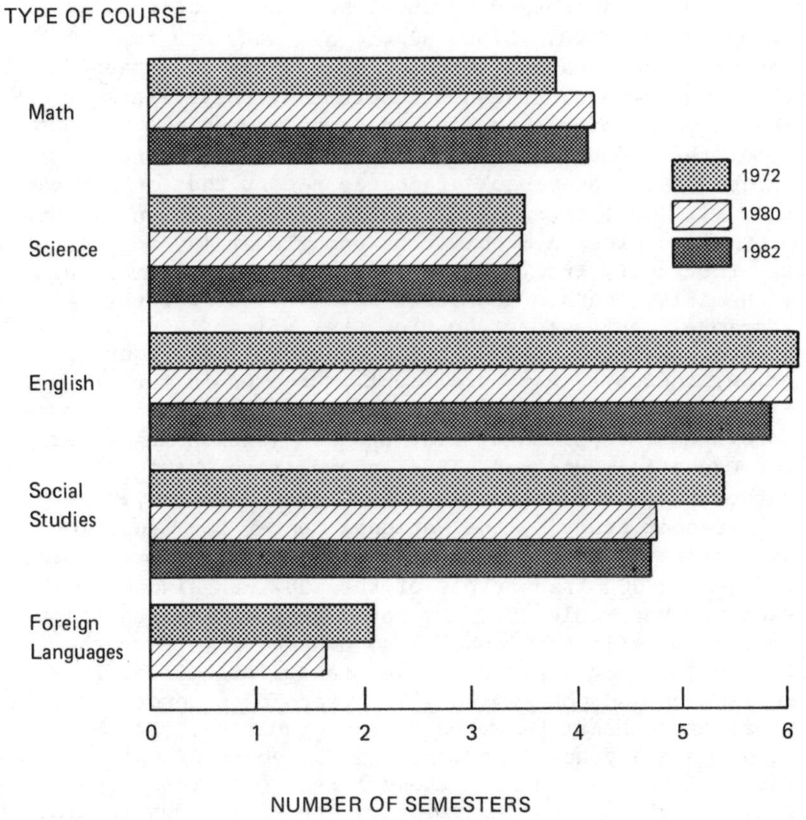

FIGURE 4 Courses reported taken in grades 10-12 by 1972, 1980, and 1982 high school seniors. Data from High School and Beyond and the National Longitudinal Study of 1972 Seniors.

SOURCE: NCES (1984:2-6); Wisconsin Center for Education Research (1984).

Education Research, 1984) are also given. Not much change is apparent over the 2 years, although the enrollment gap between males and females in calculus and total number of years of mathematics taken seems to be narrowing somewhat.

As Figure 4 shows, in 1980, students reported taking an average of 3-1/2 semesters of science in grades 10-12, about the same as in 1972. The amount of mathematics reported has increased by about half a semester to 4+ semesters in 1980. Since almost all students report that they take mathematics in grade 9 as well, this means that, on average, students report that they take more than 3 years of mathematics in secondary school. Since about three-fourths of all students take a science course in grade 9, high school graduates report that on average they will have taken nearly 2-1/2 years of science. Some of the increase in mathematics enrollment may be due to the fact that, from 1972 to 1980, high school remedial mathematics courses increased from 4 to 30 percent (National Center for Education Statistics, 1984b), however, data on college-bound students (see Figure 7, below) indicate that enrollment increased in the higher-level courses as well. Preliminary data on course enrollments reported by 1982 seniors (Wisconsin Center for Education Research, 1984) show little change in mathematics or science since 1980 (see Figure 4).

A recent study by the National Center for Education Statistics (1984b) examined enrollment data from a sample of over 12,000 transcripts of the 1982 HSB high school seniors (see Table 20). As noted above, the transcripts tended to reflect somewhat less course work taken than the seniors had reported. The transcripts of the 1982 seniors showed, on average, 2.2 years of science and 2.7 years of mathematics taken during grades 9-12, rather than the 2.5 years of science and 3+ years of mathematics reported by the students themselves. Differences by selected student characteristics are also shown in Table 20.

Data from National Assessment of Educational Progress (1983), shown in Table 21, appear to confirm that increases in mathematics enrollment may have come about in part through increased enrollment in general and remedial mathematics, but there has also been a sizable increase of enrollment in computer courses. It should be noted that differences in mathematics enrollment between whites and blacks and males and females persist, although they have narrowed somewhat (National Assessment of Educational Progress, 1983): in 1982, the percentage of students taking at least one-half year of trigonometry was 14.9 for whites and 8.2 for blacks, 15.0 for males and 12.7 for females; for precalculus/calculus, it was 4.4 for whites and 2.8 for blacks, 4.7 for males and 3.6 for females; for computer courses, it was 9.6 for whites and 11.3 for blacks, 11.1 for males and 8.6 for females.

TABLE 20 Average Number of Years of Science and Mathematics in Grades 9-12 by 1982 Seniors, by Selected Characteristics of Students

Subgroup	Science	Mathematics	Sample Size
All students	2.2	2.7	12,116
Sex			
Male	2.4	2.7	5,914
Female	2.1	2.6	6,202
Race/ethnicity			
Hispanic	1.9	2.4	2,420
Black	2.1	2.6	1,599
American Indian	2.0	2.3	173
Asian American	2.7	3.2	327
White	2.3	2.7	7,497
High school program[a]			
Academic	2.9	3.3	5,356
General	2.1	2.5	3,710
Vocational	1.7	2.2	2,744
Region			
New England	2.6	3.0	623
Middle Atlantic	2.6	2.9	2,154
South Atlantic	2.3	2.7	1,673
East south central	2.2	2.5	562
West south central	2.3	2.8	1,334
East north central	2.0	2.5	2,571
West north central	2.3	2.7	901
Mountain	2.1	2.4	543
Pacific	1.8	2.6	1,755

NOTE: Transcript data from High School and Beyond.

[a]Based on student self-reports in 1980.

SOURCE: National Center for Education Statistics (1984b).

Enrollment results derived from the 1982 High School and Beyond follow-up data are quite similar to the NAEP data.

A recent study (Welch et al., 1983) of enrollment in science courses in grades 7-12, including private schools, found that 56 percent of students in grades 10-12 were

TABLE 21 Percentages of 17-Year-Olds Who Have Completed at Least One-Half Year of Specific Courses

Course	1978	1982
General or business mathematics	45.6	50.0
Pre-algebra	45.8	44.3
Algebra	72.1	70.9
Geometry	51.3	51.8
Algebra 2	36.9	38.4
Trigonometry	12.9	13.8
Pre-calculus/calculus	3.9	4.2
Computer science	5.0	9.7

SOURCE: National Assessment of Educational Progress (1983:3)

enrolled in science in 1981-1982, up 4 percent from 1976-1977; the percentage of students taking science in grades 7-9 has remained relatively stable at 86 percent of the total population. While recent trends may be encouraging, science enrollments are still much lower than they were in the early 1960s, when science and mathematics was emphasized in the schools in response to the launching of Sputnik by the Union of Soviet Socialist Republics. Total enrollment in eight science courses--general science, biology, botany, zoology, physiology, earth science, chemistry, and physics--in grades 9-12 between 1949 and 1982 as a percentage of all students enrolled is shown in Figure 5; these courses make up about three-fourths of the total science enrollments in these grades. There are sizable regional variations in the percentage of students taking science, with enrollments consistently higher in the northeast than elsewhere (see Figure 6). For all regions except the northeast, 10th grade is the last year that the preponderance of students take a science course.

The preparation of college-bound students is of interest because it is related to their future education and choice of majors, and thus to the potential future supply of scientists and engineers. Enrollment data for students participating in the Admissions Testing Program of the College Board (1973-1984)--about one-third of all

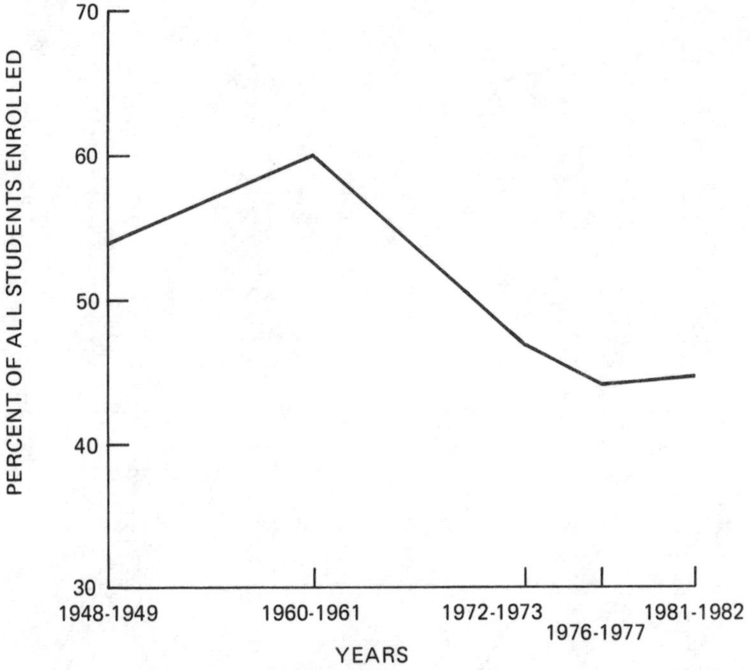

FIGURE 5 Percentage of total enrollment in eight science courses (general science, biology, botany, zoology, physiology, earth science, chemistry, and physics)--grades 9-12, 1948-1949 to 1981-1982.

SOURCE: Welch et al. (1983).

high school seniors--show considerably more mathematics and science for these students than for all students: the mean number of years of mathematics studied in grades 9-12 is 3.62, and mean number of years of science studied is 3.25. The number of years of mathematics and of physical science being studied by these students has increased steadily between 1973 and 1983 (see Figure 7). Males still enroll in more mathematics courses than do females, although the gap, at least for college-bound students, has been narrowing: in 1973, 60 percent of males and 37 percent of females taking the Scholastic Aptitude Tests (SATs) reported expecting to complete 4 or more years of mathematics in high school; in 1983, the percentages were 71 for males and 57 for females.

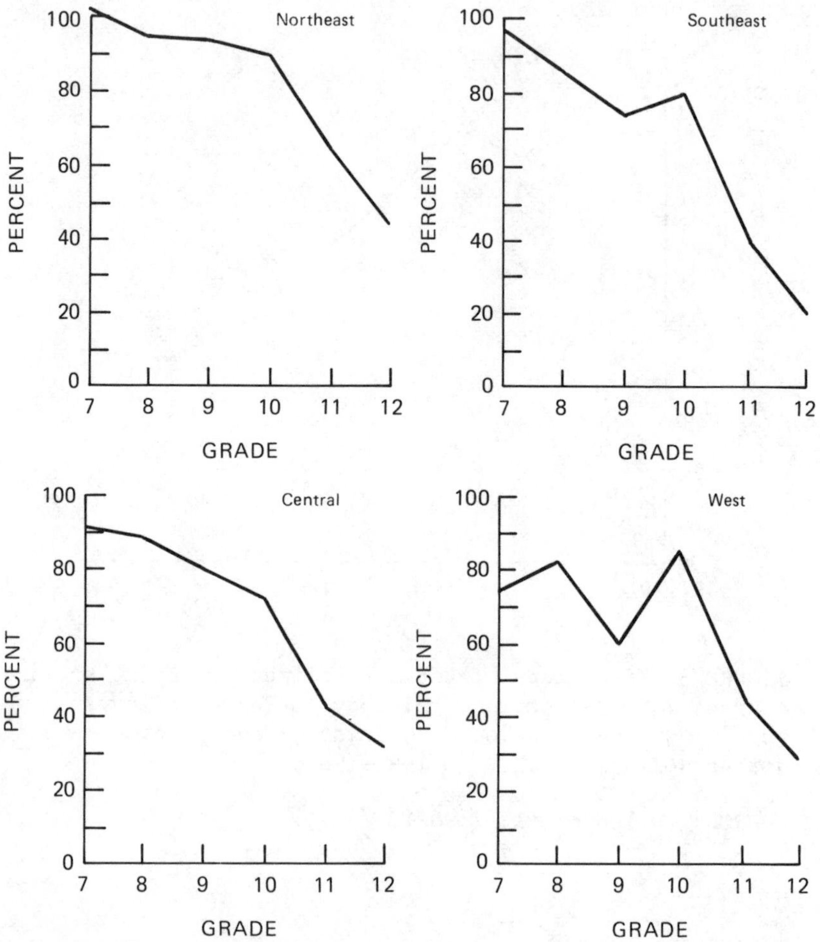

FIGURE 6 Percentage of grade enrolled in science courses, by region; special survey of 16,000 students in 600 secondary schools.

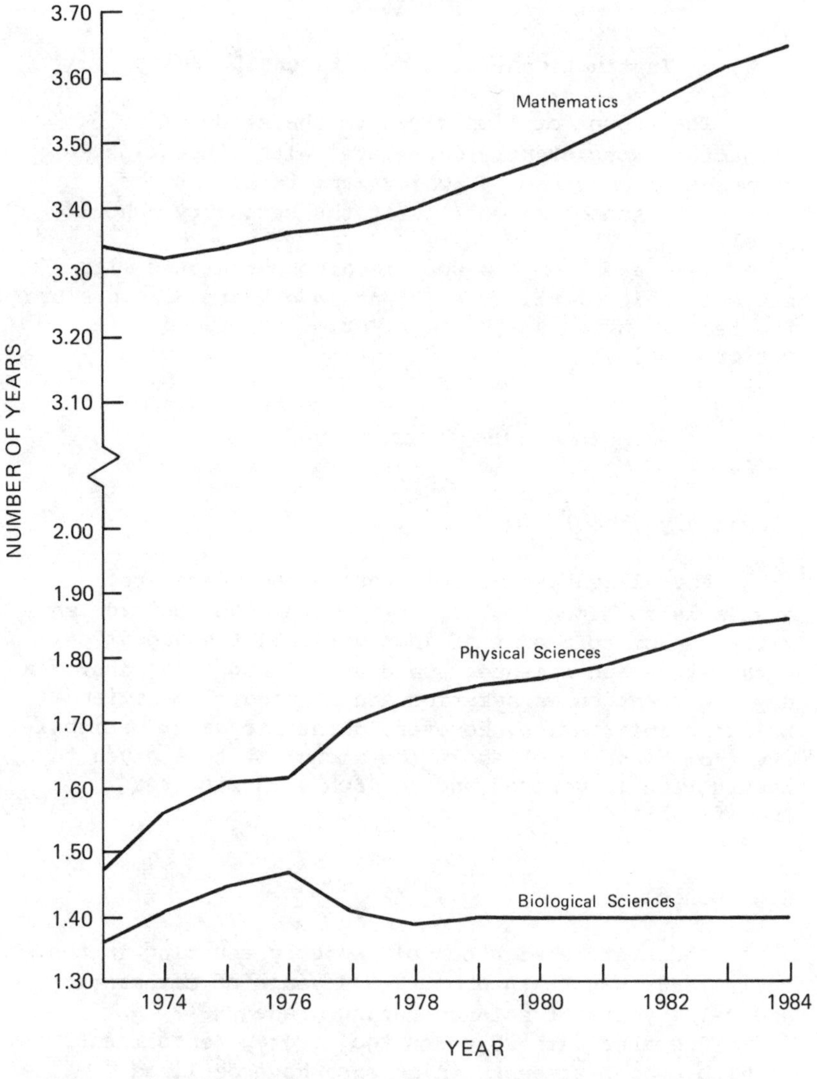

FIGURE 7 Number of years of selected subjects studied by college students taking scholastic aptitude tests.

SOURCE: Admissions Testing Program of the College Board (1973-1984).

FINDINGS

Instructional Time and Student Learning

• The amount of time given to the study of a subject is consistently correlated with student performance as measured by achievement tests, at the elementary school as well as at the secondary school level.

• Time spent on homework is also correlated with student achievement. The attention paid to homework by the teacher affects its contribution to student performance.

Measuring Instructional Time

Elementary School

• For elementary schools, not enough data are available to discern clear trends over the last 20 years with respect to amount of instructional time spent on mathematics and science. On average, about 45 minutes a day are spent on mathematics and 20 minutes on science. Existing information, however, points to great variability from class to class in the amount of time given to instruction in general and to each academic area specifically.

High School

• The average high school senior graduating in the early 1980s has taken about 2-3/4 years of mathematics and 2-1/4 years of science during grades 9-12.

• Compared with 20 years ago, average enrollments of high school students in science have declined. While this trend now appears to be reversing, enrollments have not returned to the level of the early 1960s.

• High school enrollments in mathematics have increased over the last decade by about a semester.

• College-bound students are taking more mathematics and physical science courses in secondary school than they did 10 years ago, and the increases were continuous throughout that period. The gap in enrollment between males and females in advanced mathematics courses is narrowing.

• A number of problems attend enrollment data currently available: uncertainties generated by using self-reports, differences in questions and method from survey to survey, and ambiguities created by similar course titles in mathematics that refer to different content or different levels of instruction.

CONCLUSIONS AND RECOMMENDATIONS

Elementary School

Measures of Instructional Time

• The average amount of time per week spent on mathematics instruction and on science instruction should be measured periodically for samples of elementary schools. This measure would serve as an indicator of length of exposure to pertinent subject matter; values can be compared for different years. Care must be taken, however, to ensure common understandings in collecting measures of time as to what constitutes science or mathematics instruction. Time given to mathematics or science, expressed as a percent of all instructional time, would indicate the priority given to these fields.

• Efficiency of instruction should be assessed by comparing allocated time with instructional time and with time that is actually spent on learning tasks that appear to engage students, as established by observation.

• Time spent on science and mathematics instruction in elementary school should be tracked on a sample basis at the national, state, and local levels. Logs kept by teachers could be used for this purpose, with selective classroom observation employed to check their accuracy.

Improving Methods for Collecting Information

• Time allocated by the teacher to instruction is not equivalent to time actually spent by the student. Classroom observation is needed to differentiate between the two. Time spent on such different components of instruction as laboratory work, lecturing, and review of text or homework may also affect student outcomes. Case studies that document use of instructional time are expensive, but this variable has proven to be a sufficiently potent mediator of learning that the investment appears warranted.

• Experimentation and research should be carried out to develop a proxy measure for time spent on instruction that would permit collecting the pertinent information at reasonable costs.

• Further documentation is needed to establish the variability of time spent on instruction over classes and over calendar time. The results of such documentation should serve to establish the extent and periodicity of data collection needed for this indicator.

Secondary School

Measures of Course Enrollment

• For grades 7 to 12, enrollments in mathematics and science courses at each grade level and cumulatively for the 6 years of secondary school or for the 3 or 4 years of senior high school should be systematically collected and recorded. (See the pertinent recommendation in the section on content in Chapter 2.) Alternatively, the mean number of years of mathematics or science taken or percentages of students taking 1, 2, or 3 or more years of such courses can be used as a measure.

• The disparities in mathematics and science enrollment among various population groups warrant continued monitoring, so that distributional inequities can be addressed. National data on student enrollments collected in connection with the periodic surveys recommended above may be insufficient for this purpose. States should consider biennial or triannual collection of enrollment data by gender, by ethnicity, and by density of the school population.

Improving Measures of Course Enrollment

• Comparisons of enrollment over time are likely to be of great interest, but high-quality data are needed. Obtaining such data requires consistency in the design of surveys, data collection, and analysis. It also requires reduction of current ambiguities, for example, using a standardized system for describing courses, relying on transcripts or school enrollment logs rather than on student self-reports, and sampling a comparable universe from study to study.

- The periodic studies of high school students have provided useful information, but greater effort should be directed toward reducing methodological dissimilarities. Also, the time between studies sometimes has been too long. Surveys of the type represented by High School and Beyond and NAEP should be repeated no less than every 4 years.
- Time spent on homework in mathematics and science should be documented at all levels of education. Studies need to record how homework is used to support in-class instruction in order to prompt the use of better measures of total learning time in each grade.

Assessing the Effects of Policy Changes

- Many states are increasing requirements for high school graduation; some state university systems are increasing requirements for admission. The effects of these policy changes on student enrollment in high school mathematics and science courses and on the content of these courses should be monitored.

5
Student Outcomes

The main reason for investing in formal education is to enable individuals to acquire knowledge, abilities, and skills needed for their working and personal lives and for functioning effectively in society. Proficiency in mathematics and science is deemed essential for both these objectives. Therefore, measures of student achievement in those fields should be used as primary indicators of the condition of mathematics and science education. Most of this chapter is devoted to those indicators.

A second goal of mathematics and science education, often stated by teachers and curriculum guidelines, is to develop positive attitudes toward those fields and toward careers in them. The first section of this chapter indicates some of the reasons that the committee decided not to emphasize indicators representing these variables in this report.

STUDENT ATTITUDES

Both NAEP and IEA collect information from students on their attitudes toward mathematics and science. Mathematics seems to be better liked than most subjects, but its average popularity drops as students grow older. Science appears to be one of the least liked subjects in school, but its average popularity increases somewhat as students grow older. Table 22 gives information on the relative popularity of the major school subjects.

The relatively weak relationships established so far between the liking of a subject and achievement in it were discussed in Chapter 2. A second possible reason for tracking student attitudes is that they might affect choices of college majors and future careers. However,

TABLE 22 Percentages of Students Naming Various Subjects in School as Their Favorite, Ages 9, 13, 17

Subject	Age 9	Age 13	Age 17
Science	6	11	12
Mathematics	48	30	18
English/language arts	24	15	16
Social studies	3	13	13
Other	19	31	41
	100	100	100

SOURCE: National Assessment of Educational Progress (1979:5).

according to data from the 1981-1982 national assessment in science (Hueftle et al., 1983), attitudes toward science and choices of college majors may be formed somewhat independently and influenced by different factors. Between 1977 and 1982, favorable student attitudes toward science classes went up nearly 1 percentage point (from 46.8 to 47.7); favorable attitudes towards science teachers increased by over 2 percentage points (from 63.6 to 65.9); and favorable attitudes regarding science careers increased by over 4 percentage points (from 47.8 to 52.2). Yet favorable attitudes regarding the value of science fell nearly 7 percentage points (from 68.4 to 61.8).

Choices of college majors may well be strongly influenced by the perception of students of labor market demands. For example, computer sciences and engineering have been increasing in popularity, while other sciences, mathematics, and education have been decreasing. Table 23 shows the responses of 1980 and 1982 high school seniors to the question: "Indicate the field that comes closest to what you would most like to study in college." All students were asked this question except those who responded that they were not planning to go to college any time in the future (19.8 percent in 1980 and 18.5 percent in 1982); of those asked the question, about 60 percent responded in 1980 and 63 percent responded in 1982. The changes from 1980 to 1982 appear to continue trends established in the 1970s. A comparison (National Center for Education Statistics, 1984c) of 1972 and 1980

TABLE 23 Choices of Field of Study in College by 1980 and 1982 High School Seniors

Field	Percent Naming Field 1980	1982
Biological sciences	2.6	2.0
Computer and information sciences	4.4	8.5
Engineering	9.0	9.6
Mathematics	1.0	0.7
Physical sciences	1.8	1.5
Psychology	2.8	2.2
Social sciences	4.6	3.3
Business	20.1	20.8
Education	5.6	4.0
Health occupations or health sciences	8.8	9.3
Preprofessional (law, medicine, dentistry, etc.)	6.3	5.8
Other	33.3	32.3
	100.0	100.0

SOURCE: Prepared for the committee by Lyle V. Jones, based on a special analysis of HSB data.

high school seniors planning to go to college immediately after graduation shows an increase of more than 4 percentage points for those selecting engineering as their college field of study (8 for males and 2 for females) and of almost 3 percentage points for those selecting computer sciences (almost equal for males and females). The selection of other sciences and of education dropped, decreasing by nearly 6 percentage points for the latter.

Further research could help to establish the extent to which schooling affects student attitudes towards mathematics and science and preference for a college major, as well as the significance of attitudes for such goals as improved student achievement, future performance, and eventual career choice.

STUDENT ACHIEVEMENT

In his examination of student achievement in mathematics and science, Jones (1981) found that the average test scores for all students had declined steadily between the early 1960s and the late 1970s, but that the average test scores in mathematics and science of high school seniors who intended to go to college and major in those fields had remained quite stable. Accordingly, in this section student achievement is discussed separately with respect to results of tests of nationally representative samples of students and of college-bound students. Before the discussion of test results, however, measures of achievement and their limitations are considered.

Measures of Achievement

Grades

The measure of achievement most widely used in American schools is the grade assigned by the teacher at the end of a course of instruction. Grade-point averages are used to assign class rankings to students and are given consideration by college officials in deciding who should be admitted to their institution. However, there are no established standards for the awarding of grades; therefore, while grades may provide some sense of the different performances of students within the same class, the meaning of a specific grade is likely to vary from class to class, from school to school, from region to region, from year to year. Students with high grades would be expected to have relatively high grades were they in different places or at different times, but identical grades clearly do not imply identical performances. Hence, grades are not satisfactory to compare the achievement of students in different geographic areas or over time. Some university admissions offices maintain data banks that compare high school grades with university performance and then use the results to calibrate the grading in the high schools. While such information might be a source of data about grading practices, at best the information would be applicable only to a highly selective sample of schools.

Test Scores

One measure that has come to be used for assessing educational performance is the score attained on the College Board's Scholastic Aptitude Tests (SATs). SAT scores are not appropriate for use as indicators of school achievement for all students, however, because the tests are taken by only about one-third of any relevant student cohort. And since students select themselves to take SATs, that one-third is representative neither of the student body as a whole nor even of that portion planning to enter post-secondary education. Moreover, the factors that affect student self-selection may well change over time, leading to difficulties in temporal comparisons of SAT scores. This possible variation may be true even for students who score in the top range (700-800), which would make questionable the use of the number of students in the top range as an indication of change in educational performance of the most able students (see The Chronicle of Higher Education, 1983).

At the national level, there are three sources of information on general student achievement in science and in mathematics: the NAEP results; results from the longitudinal studies sponsored by NCES (including the High School and Beyond survey of 1980 seniors and sophomores and of 1982 seniors and the longitudinal study of 1972 seniors); and, for college-bound students, the achievement tests administered by the College Board and the American College Testing Program. A variety of standardized tests and specially constructed tests are used in state assessments (see Table 5, in Chapter 3, for a listing of states that mandate assessment; see Table A3, in the Appendix, for examples of such testing). Many of the larger local school districts also construct their own tests within state guidelines.

At the international level, IEA conducts assessments at several age levels and for key instructional areas. Unfortunately, the most recent published IEA findings on mathematics achievement in various countries are 20 years old, and the IEA science results date back to 1970. A second round of assessments of student achievement in both fields is currently under way; preliminary results are reviewed below, following a brief discussion of the limitations of test scores as measures of student achievement.

Limitations of Achievement Tests

The most serious criticism leveled against commonly used achievement tests is that they do not test knowledge that is considered by experts in the field to be important for students to know; for example, the kind of mathematics that will be needed in a society with universal access to calculators.

A further criticism is that tests do not always correspond to the course content that students have had an opportunity to learn. It seems appropriate for tests to be based on contemporary knowledge and skills and also test what has been taught: yet these may be incompatible demands. With some tests, neither objective may be satisfied. The possible discrepancies between subject matter to which students have been exposed and topics included on commonly used standardized tests in mathematics have already been discussed. Many state-constructed tests do sample the curriculum, and NAEP and the High School and Beyond study also have tried to cover a common core of knowledge expected of students at the educational levels being assessed. The need to base tests on what almost all students are likely to have learned in their classes eliminates the possibility of assessing achievement not deemed part of the common core. Consequently, especially in the case of national assessments, few of the mathematics topics taught beyond 10th grade are included, and science topics tested tend also to sample what is deemed to be a common core in the biological and physical sciences. State-constructed tests may be more specific, but specificity introduces variability, which means that results cannot be compared or aggregated for purposes of reporting on a nationwide basis.

Assessment programs often serve several different purposes, for which the tests used may be more or less appropriate. Tests are used to assess the level of student performance; to determine whether a defined degree of competency has been reached; to compare state or district results with national results or with results from other districts or geographic areas; to assess the performance of teachers and school systems; and to validate curriculum guidelines. For several of these purposes, comparisons over time are of interest; such comparisons require inclusion of some of the same test items from year to year. For other purposes, test items need to be changed to reflect new curricula, making the results of such tests less appropriate for use in comparisons over time.

Other issues have been raised with respect to widely used standardized achievement tests (Tyler and White, 1979; Wigdor and Garner, 1982). Norm-referenced tests, which relate individual raw test scores to the scores of a comparison group, provide data that make possible the ranking of test-takers. Such tests have been criticized because they tend to concentrate on items common to the instruction of large numbers of students and on items that result in maximum spread among scores. Hence, they are less useful in determining what indivuals do and do not know. Domain- or criterion-referenced tests--to sample the total domain of instruction in a given subject--have been advocated as an alternative. One difficulty with this approach is to construct test questions that will provide adequate coverage; another difficulty is to establish the criterion that indicates acceptable performance. Despite the different frames of reference, the distinction between these two types of tests is not sharp: many criterion-referenced tests have been normed, and recently published norm-referenced tests have been designed to meet instructional objectives in some depth (Gardner, 1982).

The format of tests, whether norm-referenced or criterion-referenced, also may limit what is being tested. Frederiksen (1979) points out that, while multiple-choice tests can measure much of the knowledge and some of the skills needed for problem solving, they do not reflect all the thinking processes that an individual uses in solving problems of any complexity. Tests are needed that allow the student to exhibit those behaviors critical in doing mathematics or science. For example, students might be given hands-on tasks and their performance recorded in terms of process as well as the final answer, with the quality of the response assessed from several points of view. As another alternative, some researchers have experimented with computer simulation to combine assessment and diagnostic testing (Brown and Burton, 1978). Clearly, such alternative forms of testing imply a different level of investment in assessment than has typified past efforts.

The influence of tests on what is being taught also merits consideration. Because they tend to emphasize traditional topics and neglect subject matter of greater currency and importance, tests may exercise a negative influence on the curriculum by discouraging changes. Even when tests are designed for assessment rather than for evaluating a curriculum, they tend to influence instructional content, particularly when the same or analogous tests are used to make comparisons of student achievement over time. This may be desirable if the tests embody important learning areas, as is intended for the New York Regents examinations. However, if the tests do not tap higher-order skills, they may serve to trivialize instruction. In an examination of influences of testing on teaching and learning, Frederiksen (1984:195) found " . . . evidence that tests do influence teacher and student performance and that multiple-choice tests tend not to measure the more complex cognitive abilities. The more economical multiple-choice tests have nearly driven out other testing procedures . . . the greater cost of tests in other formats might be justified by . . . encourag[ing] the teaching of higher level cognitive skills . . ."

The criticisms of current approaches to testing are not new, and to voice them here does not blunt the committee's recommendation that student achievement be considered the most important outcome of science and mathematics education to be monitored. Nor does it imply that current assessment programs should be deemphasized, but rather that they should be implemented by the inclusion of improved forms of testing.

Achievement: All Students

Several assessments in both science and mathematics that are applicable to all students and designed to provide comparisons over time have been conducted by NAEP. Other evidence about student achievement comes from assessments in each field carried out by IEA; those assessments have been used to compare achievement in different countries and at different times. For mathematics, NLS and HSB data make possible comparison between the high school classes of 1972, 1980, and 1982.

Mathematics

NAEP assessed the mathematics achievement of 9-, 13-, and 17-year-olds in school in 1973, 1978, and 1982. The basic measure used was the percentage of students responding acceptably to a given item. Most of the items used to assess 17-year-olds involved material typically learned by early 10th grade. For each age group, a number of items were common to the tests used in the 3 years. Table 24 shows mean performance on the common items; Table 25 shows performance on all items and change in percentages of items answered correctly between 1978 and 1982.

The results in Table 24 indicate that the average performance of 9-year-olds was relatively stable over the 9 years (1973-1982); the average number of right answers for 13-year-olds increased by about 8 percent (a gain of 4.2 percentage points) between 1978 and 1982 after an earlier decline, and the performance of 17-year-olds remained relatively stable between 1978 and 1982, also after declining between 1973 and 1978. (It should be remembered that the design of NAEP is cross-sectional rather than longitudinal: e.g., the sample of 13-year-olds tested in 1982 does not consist of the same students as the sample of 9-year-olds tested 4 years earlier.) Table 25 also gives an overview by selected characteristics of the participants, showing that greater gains were made between 1978 and 1982 by black and Hispanic students than by white students.

While the gains made by the younger students are encouraging, a more detailed analysis by items that assess different types of skills led NAEP researchers (National Assessment of Educational Progress, 1983:9) to conclude that "students improved most on easier knowledge and skill exercises, least on those that required a more complete grasp of mathematics or more sophisticated skills." In particular, students appear to be able to perform arithmetic operations but do not know which algorithm to use or how to apply their answers to the solution of practical problems.

Seniors participating in the 1972 National Longi-

TABLE 24 Mean Performance Levels on Three Mathematics Assessments, Common Items, Ages: 9, 13, 17

Age	Number of Items	Mean Percent Correct 1973	1978	1982	Percent Change, 1973-1982
9	23	39.8	39.1	38.9	-0.9
13	43	53.7	52.2	56.4	2.7
17	61	55.0	52.1	51.8	-3.2

SOURCE: National Assessment of Educational Progress (1983:2).

TABLE 25 Percentages of Success and Change on All Mathematics Exercises, 1978-1982: Selected Groups, Ages 9, 13, 17

	Age 9 (233 Items)			Age 13 (388 Items)			Age 17 (383 Items)		
	1978	1982	Change	1978	1982	Change	1978	1982	Change
Nation	55.4	56.4	+1.0	56.6	60.5	+3.9	60.4	60.3	-0.1
White	58.1	58.8	+0.7	59.9	63.1	+3.2	63.2	63.1	-0.1
Black	43.1	45.2	+2.1	41.7	48.2	+6.5	43.7	45.0	+1.3
Hispanic	46.6	47.7	+1.1	45.4	51.9	+6.5	48.5	49.4	+0.9
Rural	51.2	52.7	+1.5	52.6	56.3	+3.7	58.0	57.0	-1.0
Disadvantaged-urban	44.4	45.5	+1.1	43.5	49.3	+5.8	45.8	47.7	+1.9
Advantaged-urban	65.0	66.3	+1.3	65.1	70.7	+5.6	70.0	69.7	-0.3

SOURCE: National Assessment of Educational Progress (1983:52).

tudinal Study and in the 1980 High School and Beyond Study (HSB) were given a 15-minute mathematics test intended to measure their ability to solve problems involving quantitative skills; the test did not include any items involving algebra, geometry, trigonometry, or calculus. On the 18 items that were virtually identical in the two tests, the mean score declined by one-sixth a standard deviation between 1972 and 1980--about the same amount as the decline in average mathematics SAT scores over the same period (National Center for Education Statistics, 1984c). For the HSB test, as for NAEP scores, the gap in average mathematics scores between white and minority-group students narrowed.

The only complete set of mathematics results available from IEA assessments dates back to 1964. Scores for selected countries from the first assessment carried out in 1964 are shown in Table 26. The scores for students in their final secondary year (13.8 items correct for U.S. students) were for students who took a mathematics course in their senior year. The average score for all U.S. seniors, whether or not they had taken any mathematics courses in their senior year, was 8.3 items correct out of 69 items and was disproportionately lower than the scores for final-year students elsewhere who also did not specialize in mathematics: e.g., France, 26.2 items correct; Germany, 27.7; Japan, 25.3. It must be remembered, however, that in 1964 the United States retained a much greater proportion of students through completion of secondary schools than did most other countries. Differences among countries in number of years spent in school and in the ages of students in their final year also may have affected the comparisons.

TABLE 26 Average Mathematics Test Scores, IEA, 1964

Country	Mean Score	S.D.	Percent Correct	No. of Students
13-Year Olds (68 Items)				
Australia	20.2	14.0	29.7	2,917
Belgium	27.7	15.0	40.7	1,686
England	19.3	17.0	28.4	2,949
France	18.3	12.4	26.9	2,409
Japan	31.2	16.9	45.9	2,050
Sweden	15.7	10.8	23.1	2,554
United States	16.2	13.3	23.8	6,231
Mathematics Students in Final Secondary Year (69 Items)				
Australia	21.6	10.5	31.3	1,089
Belgium	34.6	12.6	50.1	519
England	35.2	12.6	51.0	967
France	33.4	10.8	48.4	222
Germany	28.8	9.8	41.7	649
Japan	31.4	14.8	45.5	818
Sweden	27.3	11.9	39.6	776
United States	13.8	12.6	20.0	1,568

SOURCE: Husén (1967).

Preliminary results from IEA's Second International Mathematics Study are available on achievement differences of U.S. students between the first and second assessments and comparisons to international medians and medians of students in the two other areas that have completed their analyses, Japan and British Columbia (treated as a country by IEA). Students were tested during the 1981-1982 school year; the two populations tested were 13-year-olds and students in the final year of secondary school who were studying mathematics as a substantial part of their program. In the United States, these populations consisted of 8th graders (7th graders in Japan) and 12th graders who had taken 3 years of college-preparatory classes in grades 9-11 and were enrolled in precalculus or calculus classes in the 12th grade. The U.S. assessment covered about 6,800 students in the 8th grade and 4,500 students in the 12th grade in public and private schools (191 precalculus and 46 calculus classes).

For the 8th graders, 36 items from the 1964 assessment were included in the second study. There was a decline of 3 percentage points, from 48 percent of the items answered correctly to 45 percent answered correctly, between the two assessments. Achievement in arithmetic and in geometry suffered the most, declining from 55 to 49 percent and from 40 to 34 percent answered correctly, respectively--perhaps as much as a half year's decline. There was a slight gain in algebra.

For 12th graders, 20 items were the same in both assessments. The data show a slight overall increase in student performance (Travers, 1984:78): "In spite of all necessary qualifying remarks, the pattern that emerges is one of . . . stability and mild gains for precalculus students, especially in analysis and in comprehension, and of more marked and consistent gains for calculus students. Our best have become somewhat better in the last twenty years."

Comparisons of the achievement of U.S. 13-year-olds with students in Japan and in British Columbia and with international achievement across the 24 participating countries are shown in Table 27. U.S. students scored on the international median in arithmetic, algebra, and statistics but much lower in geometry and measurement. There is evidence that U.S. students have much less opportunity to learn geometry than the other topics and are disadvantaged in the measurement items because the items are based on the metric system not commonly used in the U.S. Nevertheless, there is cause for considerable concern about the results for 13-year-olds. Table 28 compares U.S. 12th-grade achievement with international scores: the total sample of U.S. students performs at a level considerably lower than the median level of performance found in the terminal year of secondary school

TABLE 27 International Achievement Comparisons, Second IEA Mathematics Study

	13-Year-Olds (180 Items)					
				International		
Subject	Means: United States	Means: Japan	Means: British Columbia	25th Percentile	Median	75th Percentile
Arithmetic	51	61	58	45	51	57
Algebra	43	61	48	39	43	50
Geometry	38	60	42	38	43	45
Statistics	57	71	61	52	57	60
Measurement	42	69	52	47	51	58

NOTE: Test scores are expressed in percent of items answered correctly.

SOURCE: Travers (1984).

TABLE 28 International Achievement Comparisons, Second IEA Mathematics Study

	Grade 12 (136 Items)					
	Means: United States			International		
Subject	Pre-calculus	Calculus	Total	25th Percentile	Median	75th Percentile
Sets/properties	54	64	56	51	61	72
Number systems	38	48	40	40	47	59
Algebra	40	57	43	47	57	66
Geometry	30	38	31	33	42	49
Elementary	25	49	29	28	46	55
Functions/calculus probability and statistics	39	48	40	38	46	64

NOTE: Test scores are expressed in percent of items answered correctly.

SOURCE: Travers (1984).

mathematics in the participating countries. However, this comparison must be treated with considerable caution because at that level of education there are great differences among countries with respect to curricula, student populations, and a host of other factors.

Preliminary IEA results for the last year of secondary school in Japan indicate continuing high achievement, with Japanese students ranking second of the 14 participating countries in all areas of mathematics. A recent comparison of mathematics achievement of students in Illinois and Japan (Walberg et al., n.d.) provides further documentation. Since Illinois students perform at about the same level as U.S. students in general (see the Appendix), the study is likely to have broader implications than just for Illinois. For this study, a mathematics test was given in 1981 to 1,700 Japanese and 9,582 Illinois high school students. The Japanese sample was a representative mix of ages; the Illinois sample consisted of high school juniors. The test contained 60 items on algebra, geometry, modern mathematics, data interpretation, and probability. Information on level of mathematics completed (for Illinois students) or opportunity to learn (for Japanese students) was also collected. The achievement results are shown separately for males and females and the different age groups in Table 29. The authors conclude (Walberg et. al., n.d.:6):

> For all three age groups (15, 16, and 17 and older), the Japanese exceeded the Illinois students by two standard deviations. . . . Put in another

> way, the average Japanese student outranked about 98 percent of the Illinois sample. At the upper ranges, the differences are still more striking. Only about 1 in 1,000 Illinois students attained scores as high as the top 100 out of 1,000 (or ten percent of the) Japanese students.

These differences in achievement cannot be ascribed to different retention rates; in fact, Japan now has a larger percentage of 17-year-olds still in school than does the United States.

Undoubtedly, there are cultural differences that affect student performance. For example, pressure for academic achievement is high in Japan, as may be inferred from the amount of homework reported by students and the anecdotes on suicides among teenagers who do not gain admission to a university. Also, there is an important difference in the two educational systems: Japan has a uniform mathematics curriculum prescribed by the central ministry of education; students must take all the prescribed courses, while in the United States students may elect which courses to take.

The number of courses taken was, in fact, strongly correlated with achievement for the Illinois students, but the investigators caution that requiring more mathematics courses for high school graduation will not necessarily increase achievement because of varying course content. It should be noted that there is

TABLE 29 Mathematics Achievement Means and Standard Deviations for High School Students from Japan and Illinois

	Japan (N:1,700)			Illinois (N:9,582)		
Variable	Percent	Mean	S.D.	Percent	Mean	S.D.
Sex						
Male	58	42.08	9.37	50	19.88	9.55
Female	42	36.17	7.73	50	19.32	8.54
Age						
15	27	34.35	6.79	07	16.72	7.72
16	36	40.73	8.91	80	20.49	9.22
17 or older	37	42.58	9.34	13	15.87	7.34

SOURCE: Walberg et al. (n.d.).

essentially no difference in achievement between U.S. males and females. According to the investigators, the large difference between Japanese males and females is reduced considerably when topic coverage and motivation are taken into account. Differences in these covariates may be due to the fact that there are a sizable number of separate schools for girls and boys in Japan.

Science

There have been four NAEP assessments of the science achievement of 9-, 13-, and 17-year-olds; results are shown in Table 30. The only statistically significant change shown between 1976 and 1981 is the overall decline for 17-year-olds, largely brought about by a decline of 3.1 percentage points in earth sciences (data not shown).

From 1976 to 1981 right answers for 9-year-olds increased by 1.0 percentage point on 30 common items related to science achievement (Hueftle et al., 1983:iv). (The items dealt with scientific inquiry and issues in science-technology-society; science content knowledge was not tested for 9-year-olds in 1981.) The authors note: "This represents the first [overall] positive change at any age level in four assessments." There was no statistically significant change overall on achievement items for 13-year-olds. As noted, scores for 17-year-olds have continued to decline. At all age levels, males continued to outperform females; racial differences also have persisted, but the gap appears to be narrowing at all age levels (data not shown).

Data for the IEA assessment of science achievement were collected in 1970 (Comber and Keeves, 1973). Results for selected countries are given in Table 31. As is the case in mathematics, care must be taken to interpret the science achievement scores for final-year secondary students in light of student retention rates, which vary greatly from country to country.

Wolf (1977) analyzed the changes in country rankings that result from comparisons of the science scores of seniors representing the top 9 percent of the total age group in each country rather than those of the scores of all students enrolled in the final year of secondary school. (Nine percent of the age cohort was selected as the cut-off because, at the time of the science assessment, it was the lowest enrollment rate of the senior age group in any of the participating countries.) When only

TABLE 30 Achievement and Change in Science Content Knowledge, 1969, 1972, 1976, 1981: 9-, 13-, and 17-Year-Olds: National Assessment of Educational Progress, Common Items

	1969 and 1972 Items			1972 and 1976 Items			1976 and 1981 Items		
	1969	1972	Change	1972	1976	Change	1976	1981	Change
9-year-olds									
Mean percent correct									
All exercises	61.0	59.8	-1.2	52.3	52.2	-0.1	No items in this domain		
Phys. sci.	56.7	55.2	-1.5	47.5	46.2	-1.3			
Bio. sci.	70.4	69.3	-1.0	57.9	59.2	1.4			
13-year-olds									
Mean percent correct									
All exercises	60.2	58.5	-1.7	54.5	53.8	-0.7	52.8	52.4	-0.4
Phys. sci.	59.7	57.1	-2.6	50.4	49.6	-0.8	53.1	52.2	-0.9
Bio. sci.	60.9	59.6	-1.3	61.1	62.0	0.9	50.4	51.7	1.3
17-year-olds									
Mean percent correct									
All exercises	45.3	42.5	-2.8	48.4	46.5	-1.9	61.7	59.7	-2.0
Phys. sci.	42.9	39.3	-3.5	46.8	44.5	-2.4	63.1	62.7	-0.4
Bio. sci.	52.3	51.1	-1.2	53.3	52.2	-1.1	55.7	54.6	-1.1

SOURCES: National Center for Education Statistics (1979:176); Hueftle et al. (1983:104,112).

TABLE 31 Average Score of Students in the IEA International Science Achievement Test, 1970

Country	Percentage of Age Group Enrolled	Mean Score	Percent Correct
	14-Year-Olds (80 Items)		
England	--	21.3	26.6
Germany	--	23.7	29.6
Italy	--	18.5	23.1
Japan	--	31.2	39.0
Netherlands	--	17.8	22.3
Sweden	--	21.7	27.1
United States	--	21.6	27.0
	Final-Year Secondary Students (60 Items)		
England	20	23.1	38.5
France	29	18.3	30.5
Germany	9	26.9	44.8
Italy	16	15.9	26.5
Netherlands	13	23.3	38.8
Sweden	45	19.2	32.0
United States	75	13.7	22.8

SOURCE: Organization for Economic Cooperation and Development (1974:213).

the top 9 percent of the age cohort was considered, 6 countries ranked above the United States; by comparison, 13 countries ranked above the United States when all seniors enrolled were considered. Figure 8 shows different rankings of achievement scores by country as different proportions of the age-group are considered, together with school retention rates as of the time of the science assessment.

IEA conducted a second international science study in 1983. In the United States, almost 5,000 students in more than 200 public and private schools took part--almost 3,000 in 5th grade and almost 2,000 in 9th grade. For both grades, scores improved on items common to the 1970 and 1983 assessments; there were 26 such common items for grade 5 and 33 for grade 9. Results are shown in Table 32. However, these results are open to question because of the low response rate--50 percent of the schools in the sample for 5th grade and 36 percent of the schools for the 9th grade.

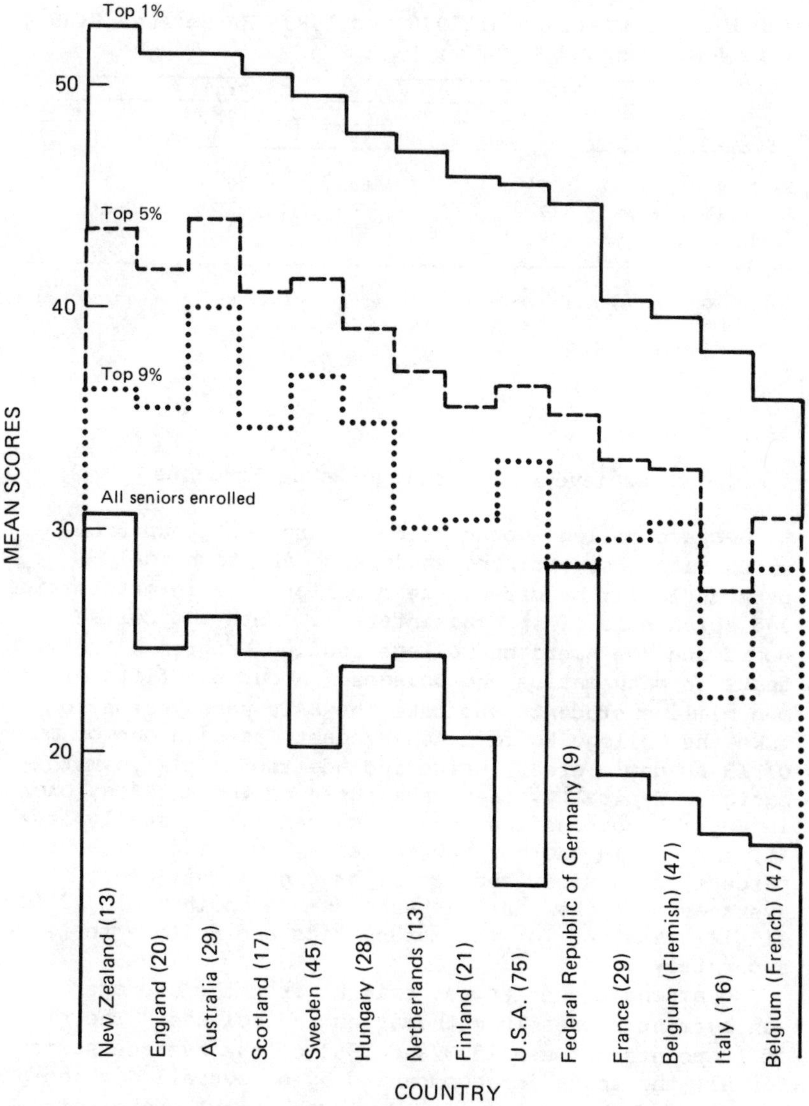

FIGURE 8 Mean scores in science of students in terminal year of secondary school for top 1, 5, and 9 percent of the total senior age group and for all seniors enrolled.

NOTE: Figures in parentheses show percentage of the senior age group actually enrolled.

SOURCE: Organization for Economic Cooperation and Development (1974).

TABLE 32 Comparison of 1970 and 1983 IEA Science Study, U.S. Grades 5 and 9

	Grade 5			Grade 9		
	Number	Scores		Number	Scores	
Subject	of Items	1970	1983	of Items	1970	1983
Biology	9	50	60	10	60	66
Physical science	17	59	64	23	52	57
Total	26	56	62.5	33	54	59.5

NOTE: Test scores are expressed in percent of items answered correctly.

SOURCE: Krieger (1984:27).

Achievement: College-Bound Students

Because college-bound students are the group from which future scientists, engineers, and technical personnel will be drawn, their performance in mathematics and science is of special interest. Both the College Board and the American College Testing Program administer tests in mathematics and science. About one-fifth of the one million students who take the SATs each year also take the College Board's Achievement Tests in one or more of 13 academic areas, which include two levels in mathematics. Typically, they take three of these tests, one in English composition, one in mathematics (usually level I), and one in another subject area, most often (about 25 percent) in history and social studies. Test score averages over the last 12 years are given in Table 33 for all 14 tests and for the mathematics and science tests separately.

No strong trends appear evident from the average achievement scores in mathematics and science. The rise of 10 points between 1973 and 1984 of the average score for all the tests is accompanied by an overall decline of one-third over the last decade in the total number of test-takers and may be attributable to the self-selected nature of this group. Interestingly, in the face of the decline, possibly due to changing requirements for college admission, the number taking the mathematics level II test has been increasing since it was first given, as has the number taking the physics test. In fact, in the last 2 or 3 years, registration for all the mathematics and science tests has been increasing again.

TABLE 33 College Board Admissions Testing Program (ATP) Achievement Test Score Averages, 1973-1984

Year	1973	1974	1975	1976	1977	1978	1979	1980	1981	1982	1983	1984
Average of scores on all tests												
Mean	527	533	531	538	533	531	529	532	532	537	537	537
S.D.	95	96	95	96	94	93	92	91	90	89	89	89
Number	294,678	246,622	228,115	228,227	212,712	208,844	201,392	200,038	198,922	196,991	192,500	198,433
Math level I												
Mean	537	545	545	546	547	541	537	536	539	545	543	542
S.D.	101	101	102	101	100	99	97	94	96	94	96	93
Number	210,734	172,032	158,061	158,327	149,918	146,426	145,572	146,172	145,851	145,277	142,306	146,693
Math level II												
Mean	NA	NA	660	665	666	665	657	653	654	661	655	659
S.D.	NA	NA	102	100	97	95	95	92	94	90	90	92
Number	NA	NA	29,334	32,153	30,497	32,743	34,513	34,990	37,592	37,603	39,093	41,702
Biology												
Mean	532	545	544	543	543	544	547	551	546	548	544	550
S.D.	113	112	115	113	114	111	109	109	107	106	104	105
Number	50,521	46,468	46,383	46,041	44,897	47,291	43,002	40,580	40,080	40,246	42,544	43,166
Chemistry												
Mean	572	581	569	567	574	577	575	573	571	575	569	573
S.D.	108	110	103	104	102	102	102	103	101	99	98	97
Number	42,863	36,521	33,056	34,294	35,009	35,007	34,159	34,473	34,494	34,888	35,728	36,419
Physics												
Mean	NA	NA	NA	592	593	591	580	592	595	592	595	597
S.D.	NA	NA	NA	103	103	106	101	100	101	99	98	100
Number	NA	NA	NA	15,644	15,882	15,408	15,046	14,656	15,897	15,991	16,507	16,890

SOURCE: Admissions Testing Program of the College Board (1973-1984).

Somewhat inconsistent with these findings are trends in the top SAT scores. Between 1972 and 1982, while the total number of students taking the tests fell by only 3 percent, the number scoring above 700 in the mathematics test declined by 20 percent. At the same time, the erosion was much greater for the verbal test (SAT-V): the number of students scoring above 700 on SAT-V declined by more than 50 percent. Once again, however, the samples of test-takers are self-selected and may vary over time in unknown ways.

Four types of tests are given by the American College Testing Program (ACT): English, mathematics, social studies, and natural science. Composite scores and separate scores for mathematics and science are shown in Table 34 for 10 percent samples of students who have taken the ACT tests between 1973 and 1984. Males generally have higher average scores than females on three of the four tests: in 1982, the average difference between males and females was 2.5 ACT score units in mathematics, and 2.2 units in natural science, about one-third of a standard deviation in natural science and somewhat less than that in mathematics. In 1984, when all ACT scores went up, females made somewhat greater gains than males, but there was still a gap of 1.4 points in the composite scores (19.3 for males and 17.9 for females), a gap of 2.5 in mathematics, and a gap of 2.5 in natural science. In science, there has not been a significant pattern of increase or decrease of scores over time. In mathematics, there appears to be some decline, possibly being reversed or at least halted in 1984. It should be remembered that the ACT tests, as is also the case for the SATs, sample a common core of knowledge in each field rather than the subject matter of specific high school courses.

Independent evidence on the quality of students who choose to go into the sciences and engineering comes from the American Council on Education (Atelsek, 1984). ACE conducted a sample survey of senior academic officials in 486 institutions with undergraduate programs and in 383 with graduate programs; the sample was designed to be representative of the more than 3,000 institutions of higher education in the United States. About 80 percent of the institutions responded. Of those responding, the majority, 60 percent, reported that there has been no significant change, compared with 5 years earlier, in the quality of undergraduate and graduate students in science and engineering; 25 percent thought there had been a

TABLE 34 Distribution of ACT Assessment Scores for National Samples of College-Bound Students, 1973-1984

Year	1973	1974	1975	1976	1977	1978	1979	1980	1981	1982	1983	1984
Composite												
Mean	19.2	18.9	18.6	18.3	18.4	18.5	18.6	18.5	18.5	18.4	18.3	18.5
S.D.	5.7	5.7	5.8	5.9	5.9	5.9	5.8	5.8	5.8	5.8	6.0	5.9
Mathematics												
Mean	19.1	18.3	17.6	17.5	17.4	17.5	17.5	17.4	17.3	17.2	16.9	17.3
S.D.	7.2	7.4	7.9	7.6	7.8	7.7	7.6	7.6	7.9	8.0	8.2	8.0
Science												
Mean	20.8	20.8	21.1	20.8	20.9	20.9	21.1	21.1	21.0	20.8	20.9	21.0
S.D.	6.3	6.4	6.3	6.6	6.5	6.5	6.3	6.2	6.1	6.3	6.5	6.3
Number	73,744	73,995	71,443	69,166	74,356	76,977	78,021	82,220	83,576	80,452	83,530	84,956

SOURCE: Unpublished tabulations, American College Testing Program, Iowa City, Iowa.

significant improvement; and 15 percent thought there had been a decline. More than 40 percent of the officials in the largest science and engineering baccalaureate-producing institutions thought there had been an improvement; these officials and deans in doctorate-granting institutions also reported a shift of the most able undergraduates toward science and engineering fields.

FINDINGS

Tests

• It has proved difficult with current test methodology to construct tests that can be used for large numbers of students and yet are adequate for assessing an individual's cognitive processes, for example, the ability to generalize knowledge and apply it to a variety of unfamiliar problems. However, existing tests of mathematics and science of the kind employed by NAEP, HSB, and IEA are sufficiently valid for the purpose of indicating group achievement levels.

Achievement

All Students

• Evidence suggests an erosion over the last 20 years in average achievement test scores for the nation's students in both mathematics and science. Results of the most recent assessements indicate a halt to this decline and, at some grade levels, even a slight increase in scores in mathematics. Much of this generally observed but small increase is due to increasing achievement scores for black students, especially for mathematics in the lower and middle grades.

• Analysis of the most recent NAEP mathematics assessment yields evidence that gains have been made on computational skills but that there is either no improvement or a slight decrease in scores on test items that call for a deeper level of understanding or more complex problem-solving behavior.

• Available information on how well U.S. students perform compared with students in other countries shows U.S. students generally ranking average or lower, with students in most of the industrialized countries performing increasingly better than U.S. students as they move through school. Taking account of different student retention rates in different countries changes this finding somewhat in favor of the United States, but the most recently available data, especially data comparing the United States to Japan, are unfavorable for the United States.

College-Bound Students

• There is evidence that college-bound students perform about as well on tests of mathematics and science achievement as they did a decade or two ago.

CONCLUSIONS AND RECOMMENDATIONS

Assessments of Achievement

• Systematic cross-sectional assessments of general student achievement in science and mathematics, such as the ones carried out through NAEP, should be carried out no less than every 4 years to allow comparisons over relatively short periods of time. The samples on these assessments should continue to be sufficiently large to allow comparisons by ethnic group, gender, region of the country, and type of community (urban, suburban, rural, central city).

• Longitudinal studies such as High School and Beyond are important for following the progress of students through school and later and should be maintained.

• International assessments in mathematics and science education such as those sponsored by IEA need to be carried out at least every 10 years.

Tests

• Developmental work on tests is needed to ensure that they assess student learning considered useful and important. Instruments used for achievement testing should be reviewed from time to time by scientific and professional groups to ensure that they reflect contemporary knowledge deemed to be important for students to learn. Such reviews may lead to periodic changes in test content--an objective that must be reconciled with the goal of being able to compare student achievement over time.

- Work is needed on curriculum-referenced tests that can be used on a wider than local basis, especially for upper-level courses. This work will require careful research on the content of instruction, tests constructed with a common core of items, and alternative sections of tests to match curricular alternatives.
- Assessments should include an evaluation of the depth of a student's understanding of concepts, the ability to address nonroutine problems, and skills in the process of doing mathematics and science. Especially for science, it is desirable that a test involve some hands-on tasks.

References

Admissions Testing Program of the College Board
1973- 1984 National College Bound Seniors. Annual reports for the years 1973-1984. New York: College Entrance Examination Board.

American Association for the Advancement of Science
1970 Preservice Education of Elementary School Teachers. Washington, D.C.: American Association for the Advancement of Science.

American Chemical Society
1977 Guidelines and Recommendations for the Preparation and Continuing Education of Secondary School Teachers of Chemistry. Washington, D.C.: American Chemical Society.

Atelsek, Frank J.
1984 Student Quality in the Sciences and Engineering: Opinions of Senior Academic Officials. Washington, D.C.: American Council on Education.

Begle, Edward G.
1973 Some lessons learned by SMSG. Mathematics Teacher 66(3):207-214.
1979 Critical Variables in Mathematics Education. Washington, D.C.: Mathematical Association of America and National Council of Teachers of Mathematics.

Begle, Edward G., and Wilson, James W.
1970 Evaluation of mathematics programs. In Edward G. Begle, ed., Mathematics Education. Chicago: University of Chicago Press.

Bell, Terrell H.
1984 State Education Statistics: State Performance Outcomes, Resource Inputs, and Population

Characteristics, 1972 and 1982. Washington, D.C.: U.S. Department of Education,

Berliner, David C.

1976 Impediments to the study of teacher effectiveness. Journal of Teacher Education 27:5-13.

1978 Allocated Time, Engaged Time, and Academic Learning Time in Elementary Mathematics Instruction. Paper presented at the meeting of the National Council of Teachers of Mathematics, San Diego, Calif.

1980 Studying instruction in the elementary classroom. In Robert Dreeben and J. Alan Thomas, eds., The Analysis of Educational Productivity, Volume I. Cambridge, Mass.: Ballinger.

Berliner, David C., Fisher, Charles W., Filby, Nikola N., and Marliave, Richard

1978 Executive Summary of Beginning Teacher Evaluation Study. San Francisco: Far West Regional Laboratory for Educational Research and Development.

Borg, Walter R.

1980 Time and school learning. In Carolyn Denham and Ann Lieberman, eds., Time to Learn. Available from the U.S. Government Printing Office. Washington, D.C.: National Institute of Education.

Boyer, Ernest L.

1983 High School: A Report on Secondary Education in America. New York: Harper & Row.

Brophy, Jere E.

1983 Classroom organization and management. Elementary School Journal 83(4):267.

Brown, John S., and Burton, R.R.

1978 Diagnostic models for procedural bugs in basic mathematical skills. Cognitive Science 2:153-192.

The Chronicle of Higher Education

1983 Fewer score high on scholastic aptitude test; Selective colleges concerned. February 16.

Coleman, J.S., Campbell, E.Q., Hobsen, C.J., McPartland, J., Mood, A., Weinfield, F.D., and York, R.L.

1966 Equality of Educational Opportunity. Washington, D.C.: U.S. Department of Health, Education, and Welfare.

Comber, L.C., and Keeves, J.P.
1973 Science Education in Nineteen Countries. New York: John Wiley.

Committee on the Undergraduate Program in Mathematics
1961a Course Guides for the Training of Teachers of Junior High and High School Mathematics. Washington, D.C.: Mathematical Association of America.
1961b Recommendations for the Training of Teachers of Mathematics. Washington, D.C.: Mathematical Association of America.
1983 Recommendations on the Mathematical Preparation of Teachers. Washington, D.C.: Mathematical Association of America.

Conference Board of the Mathematical Sciences
1983 The mathematical sciences curriculum K-12: What is still fundamental and what is not. In Educating Americans for the 21st Century: Source Materials. National Science Board Commission on Precollege Education in Mathematics, Science, and Technology. Washington, D.C.: National Science Foundation.

Council of Chief State School Officers
1984 A Review Profile of State Assessment and Minimum Competency Testing Programs. Prepared for Meeting of Chief State School Officers, August 1984.

Dougherty, Van
1983 State Programs of School Improvements, 1983: A 50-State Survey. Working Paper No. 1. Prepared for the Education Commission of the States, Denver, Colo.

Druva, Cynthia A., and Anderson, Ronald D.
1983 Science teacher characteristics by teacher behavior and by student outcome: A meta-analysis of research. Journal of Research in Science Teaching 20(5):467-479.

Education Commission of the States
1983 A Fifty-State Survey of Initiatives in Science, Mathematics and Computer Education. No. SM-83-1. Denver, Colo.: Education Commission of the States.
1984 Clearinghouse Notes: Minimum High School Graduation Course Requirements in the States. Denver, Colo.: Education Commission of the States.

Emmer, Edmund T., Everson, Carolyn M., and Anderson, Linda M.

1980 Effective classroom management at the beginning of the school year. Elementary School Journal 80(5):225.

Evaluation Technologies, Inc.

1982 A Classification of Secondary School Courses. A report prepared for NCES. Supt. of Doc. No. NCES 300-81-0132. Available from U.S. Government Printing Office. Washington, D.C.: National Center for Education Statistics.

Feistritzer, C. Emily

1983 The Condition of Teaching: A State by State Analysis. Princeton, N.J.: Carnegie Foundation for the Advancement of Teaching.

Fetters, William B.

1984 Quality of Responses of High School Students to Questionnaire Items. Unpublished paper, National Center for Education Statistics, U.S. Department of Education.

Fetters, William B., Quingo, Jeffrey A., Suter, Larry E., and Takar, Ricky T.

1983 Schooling Experiences in Japan and the United States: A Cross-National Comparison of H. S. Seniors. Paper presented at the Annual Meeting of the American Educational Research Association, Montreal, Canada.

Fey, James T., Albers, Donald J., and Fleming, Wendell H.

1981 Undergraduate Mathematical Sciences in Universities, Four-Year Colleges, and Two-Year Colleges, 1980-81. Washington, D.C.: Conference Board of the Mathematical Sciences.

Fisher, Charles W., Berliner, David C., Filby, Nikola N., Marliave, Richard, Cohen, Leonard S., and Dishaw, Marilyn M.

1980 Teaching behaviors, academic learning time, and student achievement: An overview. In Carolyn Denham and Ann Lieberman, eds., Time to Learn. Available from the U.S. Government Printing Office. Washington, D.C.: National Institute of Education.

Flakus-Mosqueda, Patricia

1983 Survey of States' Teacher Policies. Working Paper No. 2. Prepared for the Education Commission of the States, Denver, Colo.

Franz, Judy R., Aldridge, Bill G., and Clark, Robert B.

1983 Paths to a solution. Physics Today 36(9):44-49.

Frederiksen, Norman

1979 Some emerging trends in testing. In Testing, Teaching, and Learning. Washington, D.C.: National Institute of Education.

1984 Influences of testing on teaching and learning. American Psychologist 39(3):193-202.

Freeman, Donald J., Kuhs, Therese M., Porter, Andrew C., Floden, Robert E., Schmidt, William H., and Schwille, John R.

1983a Do textbooks and tests define a national curriculum in elementary school mathematics? The Elementary School Journal 83(5):501-513.

Freeman, Donald J., Bell, Gabriella M., Porter Andrew C., Floden, Robert E., Schmidt, William H., and Schwille, John R.

1983b The Influence of Different Styles of Textbook Use on Instructional Validity of Standardized Tests. Unpublished paper, Institute for Research on Teaching, Michigan State University.

Froomkin, Joseph

1974 Demand and Supply of Elementary and Secondary School Teachers. Washington, D.C.: Joseph Froomkin, Inc.

Gage, Nathaniel L.

1978 The Scientific Basis of the Art of Teaching. New York: Teachers College Press.

Gallup, George H.

1981 The 13th annual gallup poll of the public's attitudes toward the public schools. Phi Delta Kappan 63(1):33-47.

1983 The 15th annual gallup poll of the public's attitudes toward the public schools. Phi Delta Kappan 65(1):33-47.

Gardner, Eric

1982 Some aspects of the use and misuse of standardized aptitude and achievement tests. In Alexandra K. Wigdor and Wendell R. Garner, eds., Ability Testing: Uses, Consequences, and Controversies. Part II. Committee on Ability Testing. Washington, D.C.: National Academy Press.

Glaser, Robert

1983 Education and Thinking: The Role of Knowledge. Technical Report PD5-6. University of Pittsburgh.

Glass, Gene V., Cohen, Leonard S., Smith, Mary L., and Filby, Nikola N.
1982 School Class Size. Beverly Hills, Calif.: Sage Publications.

Gray, Dennis
1984 Apples, oranges, and kumquats: Comparing states on education data. Basic Education 28(5):3-5.

Graybeal, William S.
1983 Teacher Supply and Demand in Public Schools, 1981-82. Washington, D.C.: National Education Association.

Hanushek, Eric A.
1981 Throwing money at schools. Journal of Policy Analysis and Management 1(1):19-41.

Helgeson, Stanley L., Blosser, Patricia E., and Howe, Robert W.
1978 The Status of Pre-College Science, Mathematics, and Social Science Education: Volume I, Science Education. NSF SE-78-73. Available from the U.S. Government Printing Office. Washington, D.C.: National Science Foundation.

Hilton, Thomas L., Rock, Donald A., Ekstrom, Ruth, Goertz, Margaret E., and Pollack, Judith
1984 Study of Excellence in High School Education: Cross-Sectional Study, 1972-1980. Draft Technical Report: Relational Analysis Section. Educational Testing Service, Princeton, N.J.

Horn, Elizabeth A., and Walberg, Herbert J.
1984 Achievement and interest as functions of quantity and level of instruction. Journal of Educational Research 77(4):227-232.

Howe, Trevor G., and Gerlovich, Jack A.
1982 National Study of the Estimated Supply and Demand of Secondary Science and Mathematics Teachers. Ames: Iowa State University.

Hueftle, Stacey J., Rakow, Steven J., and Welch, Wayne W.
1983 Images of Science: A Summary of Results from the 1981-82 National Assessment in Science. Minneapolis, Minn.: Minnesota Research and Evaluation Center.

Husén, Torsten
1967 International Study of Achievement in Mathematics: A Comparison of Twelve Countries. Vol. I and II. New York: John Wiley.

Jackson, Philip W.
1965 Life in Classrooms. New York: Holt, Rinehart and Winston.

Johnstone, James
1981 Indicators of Education Systems. London: Kogan Page.

Jones, Lyle V.
1981 Achievement test scores in mathematics and science. Science 213:412-416.
1984 White-black achievement differences: The narrowing gap. American Psychologist 39:1207-1213.

Karweit, Nancy L.
1983 Time on Task: A Research Review. Baltimore, Md.: Johns Hopkins University Press.

Klein, Sara E.
1982 Testimony to Subcommittee on Science, Research and Technology of the Committee on Science and Technology of the U.S. House of Representatives. Washington, D.C: National Science Teachers Association.

Kluender, M.M., and Egbert, Robert L.
1983 The Status of American Teacher Education. Draft Report. National Institute of Education, Washington, D.C.

Krieger, James H.
1984 Study indicates some improvement in U.S. science education. Chemical and Engineering News (June 11):26-28.

Levin, Henry M.
1984 About time for educational reform. Educational Evaluation and Policy Analysis 6(2):151-163.

Miner, Jerry
1983 Estimates of adequate school spending by state based on national average service levels. Journal of Education Finance 8(Winter):316-342.

Munby, Hugh
1983 Thirty studies involving the scientific attitude inventory: What confidence can we have in this instrument? Journal of Research in Science Teaching 20(2):141-162.

Murnane, Richard J.
1980 Interpreting the Evidence on School Effectiveness. Working Paper No. 830. Institution for Social and Policy Studies, Yale University.

National Academy of Sciences and National Academy of Engineering

1982 Science and Mathematics in the Schools: Report of a Convocation. Washington, D.C.: National Academy Press.

National Assessment of Educational Progress

1979 Attitudes Toward Science. Denver, Colo.: Education Commission of the States.

1983 The Third National Mathematics Assessment: Results, Trends and Issues. Denver, Colo.: Education Commission of the States.

National Center for Education Statistics

1978 Projections of Education Statistics to 1986-87. M.M. Frankel, ed. Washington, D.C.: U.S. Department of Education.

1979 The Condition of Education. Supt. of Doc. No. NCES 017-080-02008-4. Available from the U.S. Government Printing Office. Washington, D.C.: U.S. Department of Education.

1981a A Capsule Description of High School Students: A Report on High School and Beyond, A National Longitudinal Study for the 1980s. Prepared by Samuel S. Peng, William B. Fetters, and Andrew J. Kolstad. Supt. of Doc. No. NCES 0-729-575/2100. Available from the U.S. Government Printing Office. Washington, D.C.: U.S. Department of Education.

1981b National Longitudinal Study of the High School Class of 1972, Study Reports Update: Review and Annotation. Prepared by Mary Ellen Taylor, Cecille E. Stafford, and Carol Place. Washington, D.C.: U.S. Department of Education.

1982a Digest of Education Statistics. Supt. of Doc. No. NCES 82-407. Available from the U.S. Government Printing Office. Washington, D.C.: U.S. Department of Education.

1982b Projections of Education Statistics to 1990-91: Volume II, Methodological Report. Prepared by M.M. Frankel and D.E. Gerald. Washington, D.C.: U.S. Department of Education.

1982c Recent College Graduate Survey, 1981. Unpublished tabulations, November 1982.

1982d Teacher Demand: A Socioethnographic Phenomenon. Prepared by Jane L. Crane. Supt. of Doc. No. NCES 381-054. Available from the U.S. Government Printing Office. Washington, D.C.: U.S. Department of Education.

1982e Teachers Employed in Public Schools 1979-80. A Report on the 1979-80 Survey of Teacher Demand and Shortage. Prepared by A.S. Metz and J.P. Sietsma. Washington, D.C.: National Center for Education Statistics.

1982f Teacher Shortage May Occur in the Late 1980's. Supt. of Doc. No. NCES 82-403b. Available from the U.S. Government Printing Office. Washington, D.C.: U.S. Department of Education.

1983 The Condition of Education. Prepared by V.W. Plisko. Supt. of Doc. No. NCES 83-400. Available from the U.S. Government Printing Office. Washington, D.C.: U.S. Department of Education.

1984a The Condition of Education. Prepared by V.W. Plisko. Supt. of Doc. No. NCES 84-401. Available from the U.S. Government Printing Office. Washington, D.C.: U.S. Department of Education.

1984b Science and Mathematics Education in American High Schools: Results from the High School and Beyond Study. NCES 84-211b. Washington, D.C.: U.S. Department of Education.

1984c High School Seniors: A Comparative Study of the Classes of 1972 and 1980. Prepared by William B. Fetters, Jeffrey A. Owings, and George H. Brown. Supt. of Doc. No. 065-000-00204-3. Available from the U.S. Government Printing Office. Washington, D.C.: U.S. Department of Education.

National Commission on Excellence in Education

1983 A Nation At Risk: The Imperative for Educational Reform. Supt. of Doc. No. 065-000-00177-2. Available from the U.S. Government Printing Office. Washington, D.C.: U.S. Department of Education.

National Commission on Excellence in Teacher Education

1984 What the Reports Said About Teacher Education: A Summary. Prepared for the May 2, 1984, meeting of the Commission. American Association of Colleges for Teacher Education, Washington, D.C.

National Council of Supervisors of Mathematics

1977 Position Paper on Basic Mathematics Skills. Available from Ross Taylor or Sally Sloan, Minneapolis Public Schools, Minneapolis, Minn.

National Council of Teachers of Mathematics
1980 An Agenda for Action. Reston, Va.: National Council of Teachers of Mathematics.
1981a Guidelines for the Preparation of Teachers of Mathematics. Prepared by the Commission on the Education of Teachers of Mathematics. Reston, Va.: National Council of Teachers of Mathematics.
1981b Priorities in School Mathematics. Reston, Va.: National Council of Teachers of Mathematics.

National Science Foundation
1980 Science Education Databook. Office of Program Integration, Directorate for Science Education. NSF No. SE 80-3. Washington, D.C.: National Science Foundation.
1982a Science and Engineering Education: Data and Information. Report to the National Science Board Commission on Precollege Education in Mathematics, Science and Technology. Office of Scientific and Engineering Personnel and Education. NSF No. 82-30. Washington, D.C.: National Science Foundation.
1982b Today's Problems, Tomorrow's Crises: A Report of the National Science Board's Commission on Precollege Education in Mathematics, Science and Technology. NSF No. CPCE-NSF-01. Washington, D.C.: National Science Foundation.
1983 Educating Americans for the 21st Century. National Science Board Commission on Precollege Education in Mathematics, Science and Technology. Washington, D.C.: National Science Foundation.

National Science Teachers Association
1983 Recommended Standards for the Preparation and Certification of Teachers of Science at the Elementary and Middle/Junior High School Levels. Washington, D.C.: National Science Teachers Association.

Organization for Economic Cooperation and Development
1974 A Resume of the Surveys of the International Association for the Evaluation of Educational Achievement. Paris: Organization for Economic Cooperation and Development.

Parrish, William C.
1980 State-Mandated Graduation Requirements, 1980. Reston, Va.: National Association of Secondary School Principals.

Pelavin, Sol H., and Reisner, Elizabeth R.
1984 An Analysis of the National Availability of Mathematics and Science Teachers. Pelavin Associates, Inc., Washington, D.C.

Peterson, Paul E.
1983 Did the education commissions say anything? The Brookings Review (Winter):3-11.

Ritz, William C.
1984 Recommended Standards for the Preparation and Certification of Secondary School Teachers of Science. Washington, D.C.: National Science Teachers Association.

Robinson, James T., ed.
1981 Research in Science Education: New Questions, New Directions. Columbus, Ohio: Clearinghouse for Science, Mathematics, and Environmental Education.

Romberg, Thomas A., and Carpenter, Thomas P.
1985 Research on teaching and learning mathematics: Two disciplines of scientific inquiry. In Merlin C. Wittrock, ed., The Handbook of Research on Teaching. Third edition. New York: Macmillan.

Rosenshine, Barak V.
1976 Classroom instruction. In Nathaniel L. Gage, ed., The Psychology of Teaching Methods. Chicago: University of Chicago Press.
1980 How time is spent in elementary classrooms. In Carolyn Denham and Ann Lieberman, eds., Time to Learn. Available from the U.S. Government Printing Office. NIE No. 1981-723-653. Washington, D.C.: National Institute of Education.

Shymansky, James A., and Aldridge, Bill G.
1982 The teacher crisis in secondary school science and mathematics. Educational Leadership (November):61-62.

Shymansky, James A., Kyle, William C., Jr., and Alport, Jennifer M.
1983 The effects of new science curricula on student performance. Journal of Research in Science Teaching 20(5):387-404.

Spence, Michael
1973 Job market signalling. Quarterly Journal of Economics 87(August):369-374.

Stake, Robert E., and Easley, Jack A., Jr.
1978 Case Studies in Science Education. NSF SE-78-74. Available from the U.S. Government Printing Office. Washington, D.C.: National Science Foundation.

Stedman, Lawrence C., and Smith, Marshall S.
1983 Recent reform proposals for American education. Contemporary Education Review 2(2):85-104.

Summers, Anita A., and Wolfe, Barbara L.
1977 Do schools make a difference? American Economic Review 67(4):639-652.

Suydam, Marylin N., and Osborne, Alan
1978 The Status of Precollege Science, Mathematics and Social Science Education 1955-1975: Volume II, Mathematics Education. NSF SE-78-73. Available from the U.S. Government Printing Office. Washington, D.C.: National Science Foundation.

Task Force on Education for Economic Growth
1983 Action for Excellence: A Comprehensive Plan To Improve Our Nation's Schools. Denver, Colo.: Education Commission of the States.

Travers, Kenneth J.
1984 Second International Mathematics Study: Summary Report for the United States. U.S. National Coordinating Center. University of Illinois, Urbana-Champaign.

Twentieth Century Fund Task Force
1983 Report of the Twentieth Century Fund Task Force on Federal Elementary and Secondary Education Policy. New York: The Twentieth Century Fund.

Tyler, Ralph W., and White, Sheldon H.
1979 Testing, Teaching and Learning. Washington, D.C.: National Institute of Education.

U.S. Department of Education
1984 The Nation Responds. Washington, D.C.: U.S. Department of Education.

U.S. General Accounting Office
1984 New Directions for Federal Programs to Aid Mathematics and Science Teaching. GAO/PEMD-84-5. Washington, D.C.: U.S. General Accounting Office.

Walberg, Herbert J.
1984 Improving the productivity of America's schools. Educational Leadership 41(8):19-30.

Walberg, Herbert J., Harnisch, Delwyn L., and Tsai, Shiow-Ling
No date Mathematics Productivity in Japan and Illinois. Unpublished paper, University of Illinois at Chicago and Urbana.

Walberg, Herbert J., and Rasher, Sue Pinzar
1979 Achievement in the fifty states. In Educational Environments and Effects. Berkeley, Calif.: McCutchen.
1985 Synthesis of research on teaching. In Merlin C. Wittrock, ed., The Handbook of Research on Teaching. Third edition. New York: Macmillan.

Walker, Decker F.
1981 Learning science from textbooks: Toward a balanced assessment of textbooks in science education. In James T. Robinson, ed., Research in Science Education: New Questions, New Directions. Columbus, Ohio: Clearinghouse for Science, Mathematics, and Environmental Education.

Wang, Ming-Mei, Hoepfner, Ralph, Zagorski, Henry, Hemenway, Judith A., Brown, Deborah S., and Bear, Moraye B.
1978 The Nature and Recipients of Compensatory Education. Technical Report No. 5 from the Study of the Sustaining Effects of Compensatory Education on Basic Skills. Washington, D.C.: U.S. Office of Education.

Weiss, Iris S.
1978 Report of the 1977 National Survey of Science, Mathematics, and Social Studies Education. Prepared for the National Science Foundation. Supt. of Doc. No. 083-000-00364-0. Available from the U.S. Government Printing Office. Washington, D.C.: National Science Foundation.

Welch, Wayne W.
1979 Twenty years of science curriculum development: A look back. In David C. Berliner, ed., Review of Research in Education 7. Washington, D.C.: American Educational Research Association.
1983 Research in Science Education: Review and Recommendations. Paper presented at the Conference on Teacher Shortage in Science and Mathematics: Myths, Realities and Research. National Institute of Education, Washington, D.C., February 8-10.

Welch, Wayne W., Anderson, Ronald E., and Harris, Linda J.

1982 The effects of schooling on mathematics achievement. American Educational Research Journal 19(1):145-153.

1983 Secondary School Science Enrollments in the United States. Unpublished paper, Department of Educational Psychology, University of Minnesota.

Wigdor, Alexandra K., and Garner, Wendell R., eds.

1982 Ability Testing: Uses, Consequences, and Controversies. Part I. Committee on Ability Testing. Washington, D.C.: National Academy Press.

Willson, Victor L.

1983 A meta-analysis of the relationship between science achievement and science attitude: Kindergarten through college. Journal of Research in Science Teaching 20(9):839-850.

Wisconsin Center for Education Research

1984 Special Analyses of High School and Beyond 1980 and 1982 Seniors. Unpublished paper, University of Wisconsin.

Woellner, Elizabeth H.

1983 Requirements for Certification for Elementary Schools, Secondary Schools, Junior Colleges: Teachers, Counselors, Librarians, Administrators. Chicago, Illinois: University of Chicago Press.

Wolf, Richard M.

1977 Achievement in America. New York: Teachers College Press.

Yager, Robert E.

1983 The importance of terminology in teaching K-12 sciences. Journal of Research in Science Teaching 20(6):577-588.

APPENDIX
State Data

INTRODUCTION

Education is a state responsibility that the states share with local districts; what happens in science and mathematics education is determined largely at those levels. Therefore, there is a need for information specific to each state. Nationally aggregated data on supply or demand for teachers do not necessarily reflect conditions in a particular state; national trends in enrollment may or may not be the same as in different states; etc.

Seemingly comparable data that are not derived from comparable samples can yield quite misleading information. For example, ranking all the states by mean SAT scores of high school seniors, as an index of educational quality, would be patently inappropriate because the percentage of students who choose to take the SATs ranges from 69 to 3, and there is an associated systemic variation in scores: see Table Al. Even somewhat more sophisticated attempts at ranking (see, for example, Bell, 1984) may lead to questionable correlations between SAT or ACT scores and teacher salaries or other resource investments. Even when data appear to be similar, often they cannot be compared because of definitional and methodological differences in the way they were collected, as in the case of high school course enrollment data available in a number of states.

The committee gratefully acknowledges the assistance of officials in the states who made data available; they are listed at the end of the Appendix.

TABLE A1 High School Graduates, 1982; College-Bound Seniors Taking SAT, 1982; and Mean SAT Scores, 1984

State	High School Graduates	Seniors Taking SAT	Percent Graduates Taking SAT	SAT Verbal	SAT Math
Alabama	49,209	2,990	6	467	503
Alaska	5,677	1,691	30	443	471
Arizona	29,849	3,352	11	469	509
Arkansas	30,810	1,221	4	482	521
California	265,843	102,261	38	421	476
Colorado	37,294	6,283	17	468	514
Connecticut	46,106	31,962	69	436	468
Delaware	9,226	4,602	50	433	469
Florida	100,936	37,879	38	423	467
Georgia	69,689	34,226	49	392	430
Hawaii	14,163	6,696	47	395	474
Idaho	12,860	908	7	480	512
Illinois	156,534	21,820	14	463	518
Indiana	79,284	37,331	47	410	454
Iowa	45,309	1,287	3	519	570
Kansas	30,098	1,602	5	502	549
Kentucky	46,831	2,920	6	479	518
Louisiana	55,424	2,743	5	472	508
Maine	16,986	7,898	46	429	463
Maryland	61,321	30,926	50	429	468
Massachusetts	85,814	56,435	66	429	467
Michigan	133,930	14,063	11	461	515
Minnesota	66,445	4,983	7	481	539
Mississippi	31,723	845	3	480	512
Missouri	67,172	7,185	11	469	512

Montana	11,612	1,007	9	490	544
Nebraska	23,827	1,388	6	493	548
Nevada	9,540	1,600	17	442	489
New Hampshire	13,769	7,795	57	448	483
New Jersey	107,550	69,741	65	418	458
New Mexico	18,535	1,497	8	487	527
New York	226,505	139,819	62	424	470
N. Carolina	73,910	34,507	47	395	432
N. Dakota	10,204	291	3	500	554
Ohio	155,499	25,042	16	460	508
Oklahoma	39,347	1,896	5	484	525
Oregon	30,480	12,708	42	435	472
Pennsylvania	168,956	87,039	52	425	462
Rhode Island	12,645	7,676	61	424	461
S. Carolina	40,601	19,957	49	384	419
S. Dakota	10,464	265	3	520	566
Tennessee	56,647	4,725	8	486	523
Texas	179,085	58,027	32	413	453
Utah	19,900	748	4	503	542
Vermont	7,413	4,028	54	437	470
Virginia	72,209	36,852	51	428	466
Washington	53,248	9,906	19	463	505
W. Virginia	24,389	1,756	7	466	510
Wisconsin	74,157	7,432	10	475	532
Wyoming	6,749	339	5	489	545

NOTE: Number of high school graduates is estimated from the number enrolled in May of the senior year. If students took the SAT test more than once, their most recent scores are counted.

SOURCE: News Release by the College Board, New York, September 19, 1984.

States vary enormously with respect to the amount and kind of information they collect pertinent to the four indicators of science and mathematics education discussed in this report. Table A2 provides a very brief summary of some of the relevant data bases that have been computerized in each of the states. State assessment of student performance has taken on an increasingly important role. As of spring 1984, 34 states had assessment programs in selected grades and subjects. As shown in Table A3, 33 states have assessment programs for mathematics, and 11 states have assessment programs for science.

In an attempt to illustrate the kinds of data available to state education systems, this appendix summarizes information provided on science and mathematics education for 10 states: California, Connecticut, Illinois, Michigan, Minnesota, New Jersey, New York, North Carolina, Pennsylvania, and Washington. These states were selected because they are among the leaders in their collection and analyses of pertinent data; no attempt was made to be representative of all 50 states, although among the 10 there is at least 1 in each region of the country. Several of the 10 states have also participated at a state level in HBS and NAEP.

With agreement of each of the 10 chief state school officers, the individuals listed at the end of the Appendix were asked to comment on the committee's selection of indicators and on what relevant state data and reports they had available. The brief summaries below cannot do justice to the work going on; the excerpts presented (with permission) from the materials supplied by the 10 states are intended as examples of their information activities rather than as comprehensive reports. Some of the excerpts do illustrate, however, instances of similarities or differences regarding conditions in a given state compared with those in the nation at large.

TEACHERS

With respect to the quality of teachers, states use certification as the primary measure of competence. As discussed in Chapter 3, this entails a great variety of more or less highly specified requirements for a bachelor's degree, usually including some professional education courses. In addition, 20 states--mostly in the South and Southwest--have recently added minimum-

TABLE A2 Inventory of Computerized State Data

State	School District Census	Course Offerings and Enrollments	Enrollment Projections	Student Assessment	Textbook Inventory	Teacher Allotment	Teacher Cert.	Supply/ Demand Model
Alabama	X				X	X	X	
Alaska								
Arizona	X	X					X	X
Arkansas							X	
California	X	X		X	X		X	
Colorado			X	X				
Connecticut	X		X	X		X	X	X
Delaware		X	X	X			X	X
Florida		X	X	X			X	
Georgia			X	X	X	X	X	
Hawaii		X			X		X	
Idaho		X		X	X		X	X
Illinois		X	X	X	X		X	X
Indiana		X	X	X		X	X	
Iowa	X	X	X					
Kansas							X	
Kentucky	X	X	X	X	X	X	X	
Louisiana				X			X	X
Maine	X	X	X	X			X	
Maryland				X		X	X	
Massachusetts	X		X	X			X	
Michigan	X		X			X	X	
Minnesota	X	X	X	X			X	
Mississippi			X					
Missouri		X	X	X			X	

TABLE A2 (Continued)

State	School District Census	Course Offerings and Enrollments	Enrollment Projections	Student Assessment	Textbook Inventory	Teacher Allotment	Teacher Cert.	Supply/ Demand Model
Montana							X	
Nebraska		X	X				X	
Nevada							X	
New Hampshire		X		X			X	X
New Jersey		X	X	X			X	
New Mexico		X			X		X	
New York	X	X	X	X			X	X
N. Carolina		X	X		X	X	X	
N. Dakota	X	X	X				X	
Ohio		X	X	X		X	X	X
Oklahoma					X		X	
Oregon								
Pennsylvania	X	X	X		X	X	X	X
Rhode Island			X		X		X	
S. Carolina		X			X		X	
S. Dakota	X						X	
Tennessee		X	X		X		X	
Texas		X			X	X	X	
Utah			X	X	X		X	
Vermont								
Virginia	X	X	X				X	
Washington	X	X	X			X	X	
W. Virginia		X	X				X	
Wisconsin	X	X				X	X	X
Wyoming			X				X	

SOURCE: Council of Chief State School Officers (1982).

TABLE A3 State Assessment and Minimum Competency Testing Programs, Subject Areas and Grades Tested, National Totals, 1984

Grade	Assessment Programs								
	Reading	Mathematics	Writing	Science	Social Studies	Language Arts	Other	Total No. of States	Competency Tests
1	5	5	0	0	0	3	0	5	4
2	7	7	1	0	0	4	0	7	5
3	12	13	3	3	3	8	0	13	15
4	21	20	6	6	5	13	3	21	11
5	10	10	4	1	2	7	2	11	8
6	11	11	3	2	2	8	2	13	11
7	8	8	2	1	1	5	3	9	7
8	21	20	7	8	8	15	2	21	16
9	4	4	3	1	1	3	1	5	15
10	11	11	2	2	2	6	3	12	14
11	15	14	7	6	6	11	4	15	19
12	4	4	1	2	2	3	3	6	11
Total No. of States	33	32	14	11	11	21	10	34	30

SOURCE: Council of Chief State School Officers (1984), based on data from Anderson (1984) and Roeber (1983).

competency tests to certification procedures. Reference to Table 6 and the accompanying comments in Chapter 3 are pertinent as a reminder of the variation among states with respect to certification.

As far as the quantity of teachers is concerned, both the Howe and Gerlovich (1982) survey and the survey by the Education Commission of the States (Flakus-Mosqueda, 1983) discussed in the report demonstrate differences among the states as to their perceptions of teacher supply and demand in mathematics and science.

California

In the past, a secondary school teaching certificate allowed a California teacher to teach any high school subject, regardless of the teacher's preparation in that subject. A number of teachers so certified are still in the schools. At this time, California is one of three states that require both a state-constructed test and the National Teacher Examination for teacher certification.

The state routinely prepares reports on the salaries and on the characteristics of professional staff. State officials have become concerned about the distribution of science teachers throughout the state and has prepared a density map showing for each county the number of science teachers per 1,000 students. Generally, the northern and eastern portions of the state are above the statewide median of 1.63, the western and southern sections below. Variations within the state are considerable: for example, from 1.18 science teachers per 1,000 students in Los Angeles County to 3.29 per 1,000 students in sparsely populated Mono County; or even between adjacent areas, for example, from 1.48 science teachers per 1,000 students in Contra Costa County to 2.56 per 1,000 students in Marin County.

Connecticut

Connecticut prepares teacher supply and demand reports, but they do not now include separate statistics on the numbers and preparation of mathematics and science teachers. However, such data on teachers in the system are available from detailed retirement records kept for every teacher. Because of recently enacted legislation providing $5,000 per year of college to college students preparing to teach in shortage areas, the state will need to develop demand/supply projections for mathematics and science teachers, including not only the numbers teaching and numbers needed, but also information on the quality of the current staff. A competency-based approach is being considered to ensure the quality of mathematics and science teachers in the state.

Illinois

Illinois prepares an annual demand report on unfilled positions. It also collects information on the number of teachers employed and the percentage of teachers who are certified to teach in grades 9-12. Since some localities--especially Chicago--levy extra certification requirements beyond those of the state, the data from different districts are not comparable. Since periodic recertification requires continuing education, retraining is also recorded. The state has not found a satisfactory answer at the state level to tracking the quality of the teaching staff beyond certification and retraining, although some local districts have evaluation systems in place; instead, state authorities work with the teacher preparation institutions in the state to upgrade their education programs. In the last few years, every state university but one has been cited as needing to improve its programs.

In 1983 the Illinois State Board of Education (1983) produced a report on the supply and demand for mathematics and science teachers in the state. Table A4, covering the previous 6 years, indicates that, for both mathematics and science teachers, the number of new teachers prepared was higher than the number of new, first-time teachers hired. Though the supply of newly trained teachers has been decreasing, so has the demand (i.e., the number of teachers hired). Although data for the Chicago public school system are not available for earlier years, in 1982-1983 10 science teachers were hired by the system, all reentering, and 13 mathematics teachers, of whom 12 were reentering and 1 was a new, first-time hire. The report notes (p. 2): "In mathematics, supply decreased by 35.5% from 1977-78 to 1982-83 while demand for mathematics teachers decreased by 35.4% during the same period. The supply of science teachers decreased by 36.2% from 1977-78 to 1982-83 while demand

TABLE A4 Supply and Demand for Mathematics and Science Teachers in Illinois

Year	Number of Persons Completing Preparation in Illinois (New Supply)	Number of Persons Hired by Illinois[a] Public High Schools (Demand) (Begin	+ Reenter	= Total)	Math Turnover (No.)	(%)	Other Subjects Turnover (%)
			Mathematics				
1977-1978	197	72 +	103 =	175	217	(8.3)	(9.6)
1978-1979	155	79 +	108 =	187	216	(8.3)	(9.5)
1979-1980	123	62 +	89 =	151	199	(7.7)	(10.1)
1980-1981	123	58 +	93 =	151	195	(7.5)	(8.2)
1981-1982	129	54 +	76 =	130	180	(7.0)	(8.2)
1982-1983	127	48 +	65 =	113	138	(5.4)	(7.0)
			Science				
1977-1978	218	103 +	91 =	194	211	(7.9)	(9.6)
1978-1979	185	88 +	99 =	187	205	(7.7)	(9.5)
1979-1980	156	70 +	107 =	177	248	(9.5)	(10.1)
1980-1981	142	64 +	84 =	148	192	(7.5)	(8.2)
1981-1982	157	54 +	59 =	113	157	(6.2)	(8.2)
1982-1983	139	39 +	62 =	101	137	(5.5)	(7.0)

NOTES:

NEW SUPPLY: New teacher graduates prepared by Illinois colleges and universities.
NEW (BEGINNING) DEMAND: Persons hired as teachers for the first time (with no previous experience).
REENTERING DEMAND: Persons hired as teachers who have taught in the past, have left teaching for at least one year, and are again employed as teachers.
TOTAL DEMAND: Estimated total incoming teachers (beginning and reentering) in Illinois public schools.
TURNOVER: The group of individuals which for any reason terminated their employment with a public school district between May and September, and did not undertake employment in another Illinois public school district.

[a]Exclusive of Chicago, for which data are not available.

SOURCE: Illinois State Board of Education (1983).

decreased by 47.9%. In Illinois, the new supply and the reserve pool of previously prepared teachers seem to be keeping up with demand."

These statistics do not take account of the new demand that may be created by Illinois' increased requirements for high school graduation--2 years of mathematics and 1 year of science. The potential impact of the new requirements is not yet known, since 80 percent of Illinois high schools currently require one year of each to graduate, while 10.5 percent require two years of mathematics;

TABLE A5 Supply and Demand for Mathematics and Science Teachers in Illinois by Main Assignment: 1982-1983

Major Area of Preparation	Number of Persons Completing Preparation in Illinois (New Supply)	Number of Persons Hired by Illinois Public High Schools (Demand) (Begin	+	Reenter	=	Total)	Turnover (No.)	(%)
Science								
Biology	83	15	+	22	=	37	50	(4.8)
Chemistry	27	4	+	13	=	17	27	(5.4)
Earth science	3	3	+	8	=	11	14	(8.2)
General science	4	9	+	10	=	19	27	(9.1)
Physical science	5	4	+	4	=	8	7	(5.4)
Physics	7	4	+	4	=	8	7	(3.5)
Other	10	0	+	1	=	1	5	(3.4)
Total	139	39	+	62	=	101	137	(5.5)
Mathematics								
Algebra	[a]	30	+	29	=	59	81	(5.4)
Geometry	[a]	1	+	8	=	9	22	(5.3)
Basic/general math	[a]	16	+	22	=	38	29	(6.6)
Other math		1	+	6	=	7	6	(3.3)
Total	127	48	+	65	=	113	138	(5.4)

NOTE: For definitions of captions, see Table A4.

[a]Only the total supply of mathematics teachers is known. Major area of preparation in mathematics is not designated by specific course or subject.

SOURCE: Illinois State Board of Education (1983).

however, only 8 percent of Illinois seniors report taking no mathematics beyond grade 9, implying that over 90 percent already take 1.5 years of mathematics or more in grades 9-12 (see Table All, below).

Table A4 also shows that, for Illinois, the percentages of mathematics and science teachers leaving these fields do not differ substantially from the percentages leaving other teaching specialities; they are, in fact, somwehat lower. Nevertheless, the number of people leaving suggests that the need for newly prepared teachers continues.

Table A5 shows demand and supply statistics for specific mathematics and science specialities in 1982-1983. Only for general science were there more new hires than newly trained teachers, but for earth science, physical science, and physics, the number of newly prepared teachers was less than the total number hired, suggesting that the need for newly prepared teachers is greater in these areas than in biology and chemistry. In general, the data in the report do not address the quality of the hired teachers, although it is presumed in the report that they have valid teaching certificates.

Michigan

Teachers certified for elementary school may teach through grade 8. Certification is based on approval of teacher education programs as certified by each institution of higher learning. The state collects information on class assignments and college preparation. Using these data, Hirsch (1982, 1983) found that in 1980-1981, 33.4 percent of teachers teaching mathematics in junior high school did not have a major or minor in the field; in 1981-1982, the percentage was 36.8. Science fared better: only 12.1 percent of the teachers assigned to science classes in junior high school had neither a major nor a minor in the field of assignment in 1980-1981; in 1981-1982, the percentage was 14.1. New state reporting forms to be filled out at the district level will elicit further information on teacher preparation and also on participation in continuing education. The state has experimented with demand projections; the most recent estimates were made 4 years ago.

Minnesota

In 1983 Minnesota conducted a survey of science education (Minnesota Department of Education, 1984) using modified versions of the teacher and principal questionnaires from the national survey carried out in 1977 with NSF support (Weiss, 1978). Some 800 teachers and nearly 500 principals participated, drawn from a stratified sample of school districts and representing both elementary and secondary schools in the state. A major topic on the questionnaires was the qualifications of science teachers.

The average age of teachers was 41, varying little among grade levels or science subjects being taught. The average number of years of teaching experience also varied little by grade range and science subject: about 16 years in elementary school, slightly higher in grades 7-9, and about 18 years in grades 10-12. For all grades, this represented about 6 years more teaching experience than the national average (10-12 years) in 1977; the difference may well be due to declining student enrollment, which caused the layoff of teachers with the least seniority.

With respect to the qualifications of science and math teachers, only 6-7 percent of elementary school teachers had an undergraduate science major or minor; in fact, more than 50 percent had 20 or fewer college quarter credits in the natural sciences. Not surprisingly, only 26 percent of elementary school teachers felt "very well qualified" to teach science; 16 percent felt "not well qualified." For grades 7-9 and 9-12, respectively, 95 percent and 97 percent had undergraduate science majors or minors, and 53 percent and 69 percent had graduate work in science. However, only about one-third of the teachers teaching earth science (grades 7-9), physical science (grades 7-9), and physics (grades 10-12) indicated certification in these areas, while about one-half had an all-sciences certification.

New Jersey

The Advisory Council on Math/Science Teacher Supply and Demand (1983) recently prepared a report that included a survey of New Jersey secondary school districts. Responses were received from 162 of the 259 districts in the state. The results indicated that most responding districts were able to fill their mathematics and science openings, but that a shortage of certified mathematics and science teachers exists in the low-wealth, urban school districts (see Table A6).

The report also provides projections of demand and supply for mathematics and science teachers through 1992-1993, using four different sets of assumptions. Baseline demand and supply estimates are based on the continuation of present trends, including known enrollment declines and increases in course requirements. Alternate demand and supply estimates assume additional mathematics and science enrollments and an increased teacher attrition rate (based on retention of teachers in 1980-1982, which was somewhat lower than in 1976-1982). Figures A1 and A2 indicate that shortages of both mathematics and science teachers will be considerable under assumptions of alternate demand, i.e., if a year-long computer science course taught by a certified mathematics teacher is added to the four mathematics courses per secondary school student assumed (by 1989-1990) in the baseline demand projection, and if three science courses are required in grades 9-12.

In 1983 New Jersey set minimum requirements for admission and graduation of teaching candidates and increased the amount of substantive study required. As a result, all prospective elementary and secondary school

TABLE A6 New Jersey, Actual Supply and Demand of Math and Science Teachers by Community Type 1982-1983, Grades 7-12

Community Type	Positions Open		Positions Filled		Unfilled Positions		Substandard Certification		Percentage Substandard	
	Math	Science	Math	Science	Math	Science	Math	Science	Math	Science
Urban	1,447	1,269	1,427	1,227	20	42	31	31	2.2	2.5
Suburban	709	644	709	644	0	0	5	5	0.7	0.8
Rural	184	137	184	137	0	0	2	0	1.1	0.0
Regional	305	280	304	277	1	3	2	5	0.7	1.8
Total respondents	2,645	2,330	2,624	2,284	21	45	40	41	1.5	1.8
State total (estimated)	4,919[a]	4,089[a]	4,891	4,028	28[a]	61[a]	62	61	1.3	1.5

NOTE: Responses received from 162 of the state's 259 school districts.

[a]Estimates based on survey results and New Jersey State Department of Education data.

SOURCE: Advisory Council on Math/Science Teacher Supply and Demand (1983).

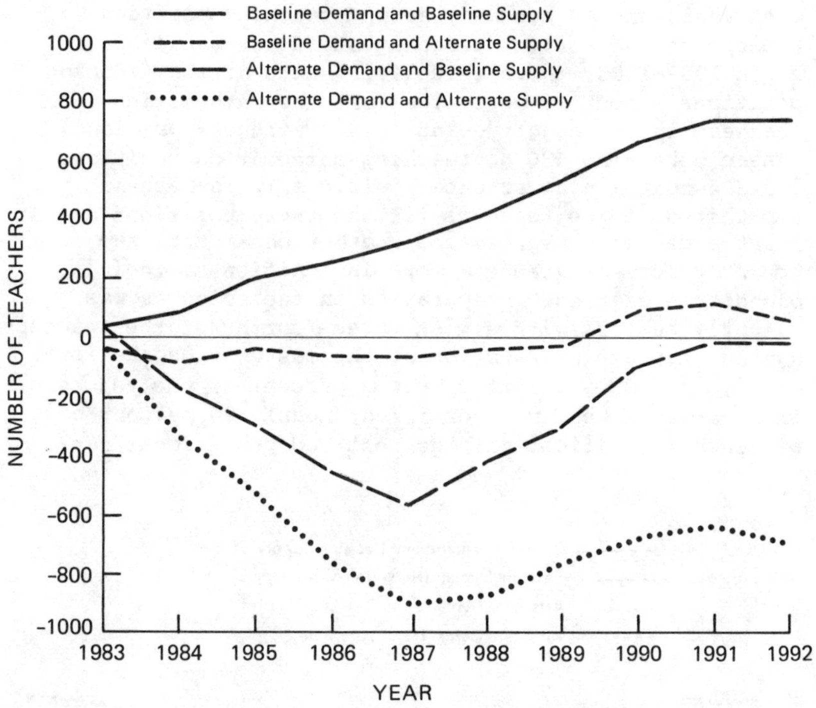

FIGURE A1 New Jersey: Mathematics teacher discrepancy analysis, 1983-1984 to 1992-1993.

SOURCE: Advisory Council on Math/Science Teacher Supply and Demand (1983:40b).

teachers must have some college courses in mathematics and science; however, it is still possible for a certified elementary schoolteacher with only three credits in mathematics or science to teach these subjects in middle or junior high schools (grades 5-8).

New York

Secondary school certification is required of mathematics and science teachers in grades 7-12 in New York. Transcripts relating to the majors of elementary school teachers as well as secondary school teachers are also collected. The state collects information on teachers actually in service, on how many get certified each year, and on how many accept teaching positions. Reports on the current teaching staff are available.

In 1982-1983, there were 14,116 mathematics teaching positions--about 13 percent of all the mathematics teachers in the country--and 11,340 science positions. (There were also 520 nonteaching mathematics positions and 604 nonteaching science positions.) In mathematics, two-thirds of the teachers filling these positions had at least a master's degree, and another one-fourth had 30 hours or more of graduate work in addition to their bachelor's degrees. Preparation in the sciences was slightly better, with almost three-fourths of the teachers having graduate preparation at the master's degree level or higher. Only a little over 2 percent of the teachers in each field were not certified; nearly 90 percent had permanent certification; the rest had provisional cer-

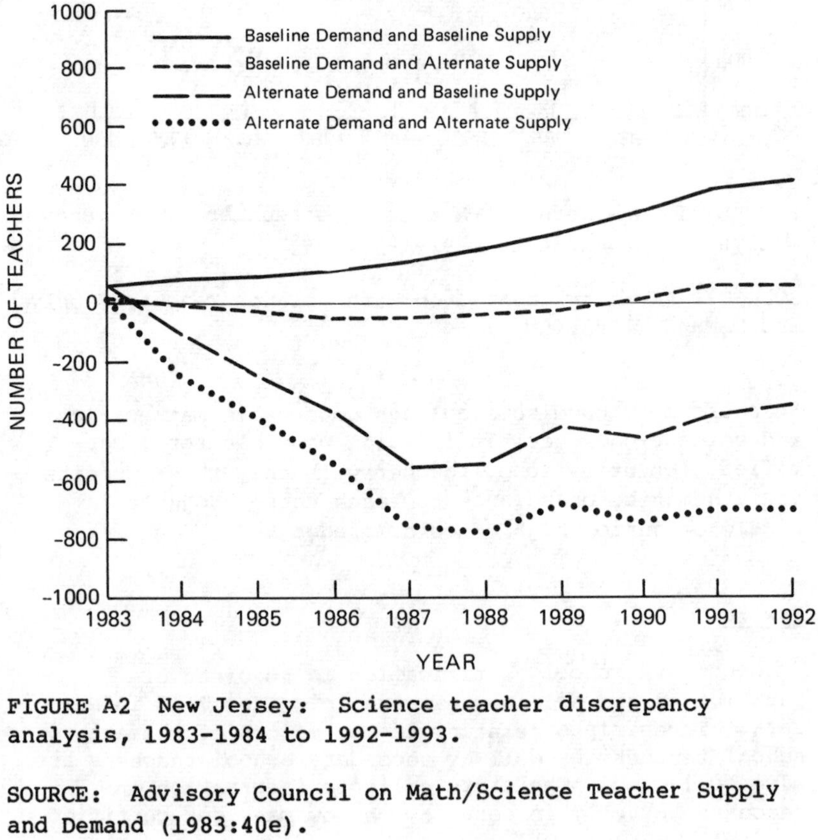

FIGURE A2 New Jersey: Science teacher discrepancy analysis, 1983-1984 to 1992-1993.

SOURCE: Advisory Council on Math/Science Teacher Supply and Demand (1983:40e).

tification (University of the State of New York/The State Education Department, 1983a). In contrast, in 1968 only 47 percent and 50 percent had permanent certification in mathematics and science, respectively. The number of provisional certificates issued declined dramatically between 1968 and 1981: from 1,920 to 351 for mathematics and from 3,571 to 656 for science, a decline of about 82 percent; the decline in all provisional certificates issued over that period was 53 percent. Teacher preparation has also improved between 1968 and 1981, with the percentage of those having no graduate work decreasing from 40 to 9 percent in mathematics and from 33 to 7 percent in science. At the same time, the teaching force has aged, although not distinctively more so in mathematics and science than in other areas (University of the State of New York/The State Education Department, 1983c).

North Carolina

North Carolina does not specify mathematics and science requirements for elementary school certificates. Teacher preparation institutions in the state vary from requiring one course in mathematics or science for elementary school certification to requiring eight in the two disciplines combined. North Carolina State University, which prepares many of the teachers for the state, requires 42 semester hours in mathematics for certification of mathematics teachers for grades 9-12 and 29 semester hours for grades 6-9. Basic algebra and precalculus courses are not acceptable. In May 1983, the state instituted rules prohibiting out-of-field teaching.

Pennsylvania

Pennsylvania routinely issues reports on the professional personnel of its public schools. In 1983 two special reports were prepared on the demand for and supply of science and mathematics teachers, based on a survey of secondary school principals, a survey of teachers, and the state's routine data base on teachers. In summary, only 7.5 percent of the principals had difficulty in 1981 filling mathematics and science positions with certified teachers; the most troublesome area was physics; biology teachers appeared to be in oversupply. Philadelphia and some of the rural areas of the state were issuing the greatest percentage of emergency certificates. Science and mathematics teachers responding to the survey had an average of 15 years of teaching experience; on the average, they took their last subject-area related course in 1972 and their last methodology course in 1975 (Dorwart, 1983). One of the reports concludes (Laverty, 1983:13-14):

> The demand for science and math teachers is unlikely to increase in the next five years. Increased math and science requirements in the new curriculum regulations, if passed, and the attraction of more remunerative positions in industry are balanced by a continued decline in secondary school enrollment through 1989. . . . The supply of incoming teachers seems to be adequate in all areas except physics; but math may soon become a problem area.

The author sees the new Pennsylvania higher education assistance program, which offers grants to students preparing to teach mathematics or science, as adequate for meeting future demands.

CONTENT

There is great variation among the states regarding the extent to which they provide guidance to local systems on the content of instruction. In New York, for example, mandatory state syllabi for various curriculum areas are prepared at the state level; other states allow local districts to develop their own curriculum guidelines and high school graduation requirements. But even in the latter states, statewide mandates for student testing, which have now been instituted in 37 states (see Table 5, Chapter 3), do tend to generate some common core of learning. This effect is particularly strong where the state offers assistance to localities in meeting the educational goals that have been set for students, as in Connecticut, Michigan, and Pennsylvania.

Connecticut

Connecticut intends to collect descriptive information on the curriculum scope and sequence followed by local districts in each of 11 major curriculum areas. Previous experience indicates that even district-level information is likely to be difficult to interpret, that information on instructional content must be collected at the individual school level. Connecticut does provide detailed guidelines in science and mathematics for grades K-12 along with suggestions for the use of the guidelines to improve instruction.

Illinois

Illinois plays a limited role regarding content; most schools follow locally developed curriculum guides. State staff provide developmental learner objectives for different educational levels, which are designed to be used as a planning tool by local districts. Decisions on textbooks are also made at the local level by committees that review the curriculum on a cyclical basis, generally every 5 years. Information on the most commonly used textbooks is available from local districts, but is not collected on a statewide basis. The state does provide free textbooks under specified circumstances: the free textbooks can be selected from a list of the most popular titles, but since schools participating in the free-textbook program are not a good sample of all Illinois schools, statistics on the most frequently requested texts would be misleading. In conjunction with its assessment program, the state collects information from teachers on the likelihood that students have studied particular topics included in the assessment tests. This procedure is adapted from that of the IEA mathematics and science assessments. From time to time, the state also uses questionnaires on classroom activities to inventory the perception of teachers and students about classroom practice; classroom observation is also used to further document teacher preference and emphasis as to instructional content.

Michigan

Michigan publishes minimum performance objectives in mathematics and science (as well as other areas) as an aid to teachers, but instructional content is determined at the local level. In conjunction with the state assessment program, the mathematics and science curricula are sampled for grades 4, 7, and 10.

Minnesota

In a state survey of science education (Minnesota Department of Education, 1984), teachers were asked about the use of textbooks. In elementary school 55 percent of the teachers in grades K-3 and 59 percent in grades 4-6 used a single published textbook/program for science instruction, and a little over 40 percent did so for science courses in grades 7-12; for grades 7-9 and 10-12, respectively, 45 and 50 percent of the teachers used multiple texts. The survey also documented the most frequently used texts at each grade level. According to the perception of principals surveyed, teacher committees and individual teachers are heavily involved in the selection of textbooks. Not surprisingly, 70 percent of teachers in grades 10-12 and 58 percent of those in grades 7-9 indicated they would choose the textbook they were currently using, given a free choice. Because of a new state reimbursement process for telecommunications software being used in schools, the state is constructing a state-approved software list that may provide further information on curriculum content.

New York

The New York State Board of Regents was established in 1784 and governs both lower and higher education. Hence, the state has a long tradition of strong interaction with local districts, including the content of their instruction. Curricula and syllabi are published in all subjects and sent to all schools. Secondary schools are required to follow them, and the state-constructed Regents exams are based on these syllabi. Although not all students take the Regents exams, these exams are generally used to guide instruction. Until recently, elementary schools have not been required to follow the state curriculum guidelines, but as of 1984 some state requirements will be mandatory at this level as well as in secondary education. By implication, an analysis of the syllabi and of the Regents exams should provide reasonably good information on the intended curriculum content for each grade and subject. Obviously, the degree to which the curriculum is actually followed will vary from class to class. The state has sponsored an analysis of 2,500 textbooks for readability (The College Board, 1983); these titles represent the most commonly used texts in the state and in the country.

North Carolina

North Carolina provides a list of approved textbooks; multiple options are given for each course and area of instruction. Information is available on selections made by local districts.

Pennsylvania

Pennsylvania's Educational Quality Assessment (EQA) taps 14 different cognitive and noncognitive areas of students' knowledge, skills, and attitudes. The EQA is used to help local districts improve their instruction; in this sense, the content of the EQA inventory can be used to help shape instructional content. Participation in EQA by local districts and by schools within districts is voluntary.

INSTRUCTIONAL TIME/ENROLLMENT

Very few states collect information on the amount of time spent on specific instructional areas in elementary school; nearly all collect information on course enrollments in secondary school, though not all do so in readily interpretable form. The data are generally collected at the individual school level. Because district organization varies--the most common secondary school arrangements are grades 7-8 and 9-12 or grades 7-9 and 10-12--grade 9 course enrollments tend to be undercounted in statewide aggregations of data on secondary schools.

California

California has collected data on time allocated to various subjects in elementary school. Mean time allocations for grade 6 are shown in Table A7.

TABLE A7 Mean Time Allocations, by Subject Area, in California, Grade 6, 1981-1982

Subject Area	Mean Minutes per Day
Reading	61
Writing/language	47
Mathematics	53
Science	25
Social studies	36
Art	16
Music	14
Health	16
Physical education	27
Other	7
Total	302[a]
Total instructional time	299[a]
Total noninstructional time	67
Total school time (sum)	366
School day length	365

[a]The total does not equal the "Total instructional time" because of adjustments for outlying (obviously incorrect) values.

SOURCE: Law (1984:167)

The state also collects enrollment data for all courses offered in secondary school and also for special classes (including some in mathematics and science) in elementary school; statistics are available for male and female enrollments. Enrollment figures for 1982-1983 show that in the more advanced mathematics courses, such as advanced placement mathematics (grades 11-12), analytic geometry/precalculus, and calculus, almost 30 percent fewer females participate than males, with a pronounced dropout in grade 11 of females in college-preparatory mathematics. The enrollment of females in physics is about one-half that of males. Table A8 shows a comparison of national and California enrollments in mathematics courses, derived from California and national samples in the High School and Beyond study.

TABLE A8 Percent of 12th Grade Students Reporting Specified Years of Mathematics Coursework Taken in the Last 3 Years of High School, 1979-1980 and 1981-1982

Year of Mathematics	1979-1980[a] Nation	1979-1980[a] California	1981-1982[b] California
0	7.8	9.7	8.6
1	27.3	32.1	30.1
2	33.5	32.6	32.1
3 or more	31.4	25.6	29.2
Total	100.0	100.0	100.0
Median years	1.44	1.25	1.35

[a]Data are derived from the High School and Beyond survey conducted by the National Center for Education Statistics in 1980.
[b]Figures have been adjusted to reflect the fact that the High School and Beyond survey inquired only about the final 3 years of high school and that essentially all California students take at least one mathematics course. Thus, the values have been reduced by 1 year.

SOURCE: Law (1984:180).

Illinois

In 1977 a statewide census was conducted on course offerings in Illinois's junior and senior high schools (grades 7-12); more than 95 percent of the schools participated. The census was repeated in 1981-1982, and these data are now being analyzed. Mathematics is generally required in grades 7 and 8, but most enrollment in high school level mathematics is elective. Many of the schools do not offer some of the more advanced courses, as shown in Table A9.

According to the census report (Illinois State Board of Education, 1980a:14), "both advanced and remedial mathematics courses show a higher percentage of males than females enrolled. Male enrollment exceeds female enrollment by 19 percent in advanced algebra, 27 percent in algebra-trigonometry, and 54 percent in trigonometry."

TABLE A9 Mathematics Courses with Enrollment of 3 Percent or More of Illinois High School Students, 1977

Course Title	Number of Schools Offering Course	Percent of Schools in State	Percent of All High School Students Enrolled[a]
Pre-algebra	110	15.6	3.2
Elementary algebra	548	77.8	12.4
Intermediate algebra	457	64.9	6.7
Advanced algebra	401	56.9	3.8
Elementary general math, grades 9-12	429	60.9	4.8
Plane geometry	466	66.2	7.9
Integrated plane and solid geometry	217	30.8	3.2
Remedial math	238	33.8	4.0

[a]The percent enrollment would have to be multiplied by 3 or 4 to make the data comparable to national data on percentage of seniors who have taken various courses.

SOURCE: Illinois State Board of Education (1980a:4)

Table A10 shows enrollments in high school science courses. Data on gender differences indicate that male enrollment in physics is more than twice that of females, although the difference in first-year chemistry is negligible. Female enrollment is greater than that of males in all biology courses and in honors physics and chemistry.

Illinois also has data from student self reports, shown in Table A11, on a state sample from High School and Beyond. Comparable national percentages are given in parentheses.

Michigan

Data on course offerings, required credits for graduation, and estimated course enrollment (compiled separately for males and females) were requested from all Michigan high schools in spring 1983. Two-thirds of the schools responded; most of those schools (88 percent) include grade 9. In mathematics the average number of years required by local districts for graduation is 1.5, and the average taken is 2.8 (see Table A12). Although, on average, 1.3 years of science are required for

TABLE A10 Selected Science Courses and Percentage of Illinois High School Students Enrolled, 1977

Course Title	Number of Schools Offering Course	Percent of Schools in State	Percent of All High School Students Enrolled[a]
Biology, first year	620	88.1	17.7
Chemistry, first year	597	84.8	5.6
Physical science, first and second year	307	43.6	5.4
General science, grade 9	291	41.3	4.9
Earth science	227	32.2	3.4
Physics, first year	535	76.0	2.6
Biology, second year, advanced	354	50.3	2.1

[a]The percent enrollment would have to be multiplied by 3 or 4 to make the data comparable to national data on percentage of seniors who have taken various courses.

SOURCE: Illinois State Board of Education (1980b:3).

graduation, 2.2 years are taken (see Table A13). In both mathematics and science, there is a major decline in enrollment as the sequence of courses advances.

Students in some locations do not have the opportunity to take higher-level courses: 41 percent of the schools do not offer calculus; 44 percent do not offer earth sciences; 8 percent do not offer physics; and only 60 percent of the high schools reported having computer courses available.

Minnesota

In the survey of science teaching conducted by the state in 1983 (Minnesota Department of Education, 1984), elementary school teachers provided data about time spent on various subjects. For grades K-3, the average for mathematics was 38 minutes per day, for science 17 minutes per day, for social studies 19 minutes per day, and for reading and language arts 128 minutes per day. For grades 4-6, the average for mathematics was 51 minutes per day, for science 26 minutes per day, for social studies 35 minutes per day, and for reading and language arts 90 minutes per day. These time allocations are virtually the same as reported in the analogous national

TABLE All Percent of Illinois and U.S. High School Seniors Reporting Various Amounts of Mathematics and Science, 1980, Grades 10-12

Subject	None	0.5-1 Years	1.5-2 Years	2.5-3 Years	3+ Years
Mathematics	8 (5)	26 (24)	31 (34)	24 (29)	9 (8)
Science	13 (9)	35 (36)	28 (31)	15 (18)	6 (6)

NOTE: Percent of U.S. high school seniors are shown in parentheses.

SOURCE: Illinois State Board of Education (1981:3).

survey done in 1977. Nearly two-thirds of the Minnesota teachers reported that they spent about the same amount of time on science in 1983 as they did 3 years earlier; of the rest, half reported spending more time and half reported spending less time.

Information on science course offerings in secondary schools was obtained from principals. The data indicate that schools with grades 10-12 only were significantly more likely to offer advanced science courses than schools that include one or more of the lower grades: for example, 62 percent of schools with only grades 10-12 offered advanced biology while 32 percent of schools with grades 7-12 offered it. Enrollment statistics for secondary school science courses show that close to one-half of the students enrolled in each subject are female, except for enrollment in physics in grades 10-12, which averages 38 percent female enrollment.

New Jersey

Beginning with the graduating class of 1985, students seeking a high school diploma in New Jersey will be required to have taken 2 years of computational mathematics (arithmetic, not algebra, geometry, or trigonometry) and 1 year of science (laboratory work not required). Only one public college in New Jersey requires an achievement test in mathematics as part of

TABLE A12 Course Enrollments for Mathematics, 1983

Course	Percent of All Students	Enrolled Students: Percent Male	Percent Female
Remedial	24	55	45
Vocational	8	58	42
Consumer	20	52	48
Algebra	77	50	50
Geometry	57	57	43
Advanced algebra	33	51	49
Trigonometry	17	53	47
Calculus	8	56	44
Other	32	51	49

SOURCE: Michigan Department of Education (1983).

its admission requirements; none requires an achievement test in any science area. Nevertheless, in 1982, almost one-half of all graduating high school seniors had completed at least 2 years of algebra or 1 year of chemistry; two-thirds had completed 1 year of geometry; and one-quarter had completed 1 year of physics (Advisory Council on Math/Science Teacher Supply and Demand, 1983).

In 1982 71 percent of college-bound males and 57 percent of college-bound females took 4 or more years of mathematics; college-bound males also averaged 3.4 years of science, and college-bound females averaged 3.2 years.

New York

A census of course enrollments is collected yearly in New York, with every teacher reporting on course titles, number of students, and type of class. Enrollment information is not collected separately for males and females or for different ethnic groups. The data are used to generate 15 to 20 annual reports on enrollment, plus several ad hoc reports. Despite a slight decrease in total enrollment, registration in mathematics and science courses in grades 10-12 increased both in percentage terms and in actual numbers between 1972-1973

TABLE A13 Course Enrollments for Science, 1983

Course	Percent of All Students	Enrolled Students Percent Male	Percent Female
General science	35	52	48
Biology	82	48	52
Earth science	22	52	48
Physics	18	56	44
Chemistry	38	51	49
Other	22	53	47

SOURCE: Michigan Department of Education (1983).

and 1977-1978. Between 1977-1978 and 1982-1983 there was a further decrease in total student enrollment of 120,000 students, but the percent enrolled in science and mathematics continued to increase, as shown in Table A14. A New York State subsample of the High School and Beyond sample provides additional information, shown in Tables A15, A16, and A17, on the number and specific courses taken by 1980 seniors in New York and in the United States. New York students who graduate from high school show a considerably higher level of preparation than do U.S. students as a whole; the state has, however, the sixth highest drop-out rate in the nation (Bell, 1984).

TABLE A14 Registration in Grades 10-12 Mathematics and Science Courses in New York State Public Schools, 1973-1974, 1977-1978, and 1982-1983

	Science		Mathematics		
Year	Number of Students	Ratio to Grades 10-12 Enrollment	Number of Students	Ratio to Grades 10-12 Enrollment	Total Enrollment Grades 10-12
1973-1974	647,754	.836	401,093	.517	775,141
1977-1978	674,126	.877	420,375	.547	768,252
1982-1983	591,445	.912	418,521	.645	648,479

SOURCE: Unpublished data provided by the University of the State of New York/The State Education Department.

TABLE A15 Cumulative Percentage of 1980 High School Seniors Reporting Varying Amounts of Mathematics Taken, by Sex, Grades 10-12

Amount of Coursework	All		Male		Female	
	Nation	N.Y.	Nation	N.Y.	Nation	N.Y.
Total, including those with no coursework	100	100	100	100	100	100
1 year or more	93	94	94	97	92	90
2 years or more	67	76	71	81	63	70
3 years or more	34	44	40	54	28	33

SOURCE: University of the State of New York/The State Education Department (1982:5).

TABLE A16 Cumulative Percentage of 1980 High School Seniors Reporting Varying Amounts of Science Taken, by Sex, Grades 10-12

Amount of Coursework	All		Male		Female	
	Nation	N.Y.	Nation	N.Y.	Nation	N.Y.
Total, including those with no coursework	100	100	100	100	100	100
1 year or more	90	89	91	93	89	85
2 years or more	53	69	57	75	50	62
3 years or more	23	41	27	48	19	33

SOURCE: University of the State of New York/The State Education Department (1982:5).

TABLE A17 Percentage of 1980 High School Seniors Reporting Mathematics and Science Courses Taken, Course and Sex, Grades 10-12

Course	Nation			New York		
	All	Male	Female	All	Male	Female
Algebra I	79	79	79	86	87	85
Algebra II	49	51	47	60	64	54
Geometry	56	58	55	69	73	63
Trigonometry	26	30	22	54	59	48
Calculus	8	10	6	16	20	11
Physics	19	26	14	36	46	25
Chemistry	37	39	35	56	62	49

SOURCE: University of the State of New York/The State Education Department (1982:9).

North Carolina

North Carolina collects course enrollment data for grades 9-12 annually and information on blocks of instructional areas for grades 7 and 8. Data are not collected separately for males and females or according to ethnicity. The data are stored in the state's management information system and are available for specific analyses.

Pennsylvania

Enrollment data show steadily declining enrollments in Pennsylvania's public secondary schools, but there has been an increase in enrollments in higher-level courses. Total enrollment in 1973-1974 was 1,137,660 students; in analytic geometry and calculus, it was 14,700 (1.3 percent of total high school enrollment); in physics, 37,000 (3.2 percent). The analogous numbers for 1981-1982 were 935,670 total enrollment; 26,000 in analytic geometry/calculus (2.7 percent), and 36,200 in physics (3.9 percent).

Washington

Washington periodically surveys requirements for high school graduation set by local districts. There are two data bases available on enrollment: one is derived from a survey of 1980 high school seniors representing a state sample of High School and Beyond; the data are shown in Tables A18 and A19. State enrollments and differences in enrollment between males and females in advanced mathematics and physical science courses mirror national statistics (see Table A20). The second set of data comes from a statewide census (including private schools) of courses taken by high school students to which more than 82 percent of the schools responded; the data are shown in Tables A21 and A22.

Fewer than 40 percent of the high schools in Washington offer calculus; some 30 percent do not offer introductory (first-year) physics. The Washington enrollment data in Tables A18-A22 illustrate some problems with data that come from different sources. For example, enrollments in trigonometry are given as 29 percent in the HSB data in Table A20 and as 6 percent (1.4 x 4) in the census data

TABLE A18 Cumulative Percentage of 1980 High School Seniors Reporting Varying Amounts of Mathematics Taken, by Sex, Grades 10-12

Amount of Coursework	All		Male		Female	
	Nation	Washington	Nation	Washington	Nation	Washington
Total, including those with no coursework	100	100	100	100	100	100
1 year or more	93	88	94	92	92	84
2 years or more	67	55	71	61	63	49
3 years or more	34	23	40	26	28	20

SOURCE: Brouillet et al. (1982:3).

TABLE A19 Cumulative Percentage of 1980 High School Seniors Reporting Varying Amounts of Science Taken, by Sex, Grades 10-12

Amount of Coursework	All		Male		Female	
	Nation	Washington	Nation	Washington	Nation	Washington
Total, including those with no coursework	100	100	100	100	100	100
1 year or more	90	92	91	92	89	93
2 years or more	53	45	57	48	50	42
3 years or more	23	17	27	21	19	13

SOURCE: Brouillet et al. (1982:3).

in Table A21: the HSB data, based on student self reports, are probably high; the state census data may be low. On the other hand, there is reasonably good agreement for some other courses: for example, for chemistry, 37 percent (HSB) and 32 percent (census); for calculus, 8 percent (HSB) and 6 percent (census).

A summary of enrollment data derived from the HSB study for 1980 seniors is given in Table A23.

STUDENT ACHIEVEMENT

Competency testing or assessment programs of student achievement have been mandated in 39 states (see Table 5, Chapter 3); 22 states have both. Most of the tests and programs include mathematics at selected grade levels, but not science (see Table A3 above). The purposes of the assessments, the designs of the testing programs, the degree of participation by local districts or individual students, and the types of tests used vary greatly. The majority of states having assessment programs list as their purposes the use of the data by school districts (25 states) and monitoring trends and progress (24 states); other purposes listed include state policy, public accountability, and national comparison (Council of Chief State School Officers, 1984).

Many states use nationally normed, standardized tests available through commercial publishers, particularly at the lower grade levels; others construct their own instruments, whether testing for competency in the skills required for high school graduation or for achievement in a particular subject. Some states test all students in selected grades, usually on a few subjects per year; some test on a sample basis. Some states make participation by local districts voluntary; some make participation by schools or by individual students voluntary. Some assessment programs concentrate on the attainment of cognitive skills; others include questions on student attitudes. Most states collect at least some information on variables concerning the students and the schools taking part in the assessment. Analysis and reporting may be done using districts, schools, grades, or achievement bands as the unit of analysis. Four states--California, Illinois, New York, and Washington--have participated through state subsamples in the HSB study, and several states have used some of the NAEP tests for their own assessments. This participation allows states to appraise selected aspects

TABLE A20 Percentage of 1980 High School Seniors Reporting Mathematics and Science Courses Taken, by Course and Sex, Grades 10-12

	Nation			Washington		
Course	All	Male	Female	All	Male	Female
Algebra I	79	79	79	85	85	84
Algebra II	49	51	47	53	56	49
Geometry	56	58	55	60	63	58
Trigonometry	26	30	22	29	33	24
Calculus	8	10	6	8	10	7
Physics	19	26	14	20	27	14
Chemistry	37	39	35	37	40	35

Source: Brouillet et al. (1982:4).

TABLE A21 Enrollment in Selected Mathematics Courses

Course	Percent of All High School Students (Grades 9-12) Enrolled
Algebra, first year	15.88
Algebra, intermediate, second year	6.77
Algebra, integ. and trigonometry	3.78
Calculus	1.53
Geometry	13.91
Mathematics, general	7.89
Advanced courses	3.04
Trigonometry	1.42

NOTE: On the assumption, not quite accurate, that enrollment in each grade is about one-fourth of the enrollment in grades 9-12, percentages need to be multiplied by 4 to yield percentage of seniors having taken a course.

SOURCE: Adapted from Brouillet (1982:7).

TABLE A22 Enrollment in Selected Science Courses

Course	Percent of All High School Students (Grades 9-12) Enrolled
Biology, introductory	23.45
Chemistry, introductory	7.97
Earth science, geology, natural history	3.72
Physics, introductory	3.91
Science, general	4.32
Science, physical	3.80

NOTE: On the assumption, not quite accurate, that enrollment in each grade is about one-fourth of the enrollment in grades 9-12, percentages need to be multiplied by 4 to yield percentage of seniors having taken a course.

SOURCE: Adapted from Brouillet (1982:8-9).

of their educational systems in the light of more general findings for the United States on such matters as enrollment in particular courses or attainment on tests of cognitive achievement.

In addition to participating in statewide assessments, many local districts administer their own testing programs. There is as much variation among districts within a state as there is among states. State and local assessments tend to concentrate on basic skills, including mathematics achievement up to 9th-grade algebra. There is much less assessment of science achievement or of achievement in the more advanced mathematics courses--understandably so, since over the last decade the emphasis in education has been to ensure that students acquire the basic skills. However, several states are planning to add student achievement in science as an area to be assessed periodically.

California

During 1982-1983 all California students in grades 3, 6, and 12 were assessed with state-constructed tests in

TABLE A23 Percentage of 1980 Seniors Reporting Enrollment in Advanced Science and Mathematics Courses

Course	Nation[a]	California[b]	New York[c]	Washington[d]
Algebra I	79	81	86	85
Algebra II	49	50	60	53
Geometry	56	59	69	60
Trigonometry	26	25	54	29
Calculus	8	8	16	8
Physics	19	17	36	20
Chemistry	37	33	56	37

[a]Data from National Center for Education Statistics (1981).
[b]Data from Law (1984:180).
[c]Data from University of the State of New York/The State Education Department (1982:9).
[d]Data from Brouillet et al. (1982:4).

reading, written language, and mathematics; these same areas and grades have been tested every year for several years. For grade 3, scores in all three areas have been going up steadily since 1979-1980; scores on reading tests have been improving for 16 years. For grade 6, there was some improvement over the previous year in written language and mathematics, while scores declined slightly in reading. For grade 12, scores in mathematics stayed constant and scores in reading and written language declined slightly. California students in the 3rd and 6th grades perform at about the same levels as the national average; Californians in the 12th grade perform somewhat below the national average (Law, 1984).

Connecticut

Connecticut's assessment program (CAEP) is designed to test every subject at 5-year intervals. Samples of students in grades 4, 8, and 11 are tested. The state uses the NAEP tests as a base for its assessment program. The most recent CAEP testing in mathematics and science took place in 1979-1980; mathematics achievement will be

TABLE A24 Performance of Students on NAEP Mathematics Items, 1979-1980

Area	Average Percent Correct 9-Year-Olds (11 Items)	13-Year-Olds (17 Items)	17-Year-Olds (13 Items)
Connecticut	72	65	72
United States	57	63	69
Northeast	62	66	70

SOURCE: Wolfe (1980).

retested in 1984-1985, and science will be tested in 1985-1986. The assessments are designed so that comparisons over time are possible. The state also administers a statewide basic skills testing program to all students in grade 9 to ensure that those who have not acquired basic competencies will have the opportunity to learn them before high school graduation.

The 1979-1980 Connecticut assessment in mathematics used some of the same items as the national mathematics assessment of 1978-1979. The performance of students in Connecticut as compared with those in the nation as a whole and with those in the northeast is shown in Table A24. A comparison of this assessment with an earlier mathematics assessment done in 1976-77 shows little change in performance for any of the age groups in Connecticut.

Science achievement was also assessed in 1979-1980; again, some items common to NAEP were used. Connecticut students scored about the same as students in the United States as a whole, but somewhat lower than students in the northeast. The 1979-1980 scores were also compared with an earlier CAEP science assessment in 1974-1975. As is true of all U.S. students, scores for Connecticut students decreased during this 5-year period: 3.3 percentage points for grade 4 (23 common items); 4.2 percentage points for grade 8 (32 common items); and 4.9 percentage points for grade 11 (38 items) (National Evaluation Systems, Inc., 1980).

Illinois

The state has administered the Illinois Inventory of Educational Progress (IIEP) since 1976. Grades 4, 8, and 11 are sampled; special subtests are used for reading, mathematics, and science. The state also conducted a "decade study," comparing student performance between 1970 and 1981 in English, mathematics, natural science, and social science. In addition, data are available from a state sample of the HSB study and from NAEP. A self-selected sample of students (66 percent of the total number of high school graduates) takes the college admissions test of the American College Testing Program (ACT), required for admission to the state system of higher education. Only 15 percent of Illinois students take SATs; the number taking the College Board achievement tests is negligible.

In mathematics, the IIEP shows gains for all three grades tested between 1976 and 1980, with a leveling off or decline in achievement in 1981. The decade study in mathematics measured knowledge in advanced mathematics of students in grade 11; results, recorded in school means, were significantly lower in 1981, as shown in Table A25.

Illinois results for the mathematics items in High School and Beyond, shown in Table A26, are similar to national results. Illinois students score at about the same level as all U.S. students on the ACT mathematics test. After a slight decline between 1972 and 1975, test results have been similar every year. Females scored consistently below males both in Illinois and across the nation.

With respect to science achievement, there are four data sources: the IIEP tests for 1977 and 1981, the decade study tests assessing achievement in advanced science, the High School and Beyond data, and the ACT scores. The IIEP data show that performance in physical science either stayed level or increased (for grade 11), but performance in life science declined significantly for all three grades. The decade study shows a significant performance decrease: in 1970, student performance averaged 43 percent (9.9 items answered correctly); in 1981, the average was 34.3 percent (7.9 items answered correctly). The decline was more than two standard deviations. ACT scores on the science test, however, have remained level during this period. The authors of the report on student achievement in Illinois (Illinois State Board of Education, 1982:58) conclude:

TABLE A25 Illinois Decade Study School Means and Standard Deviations for Achievement in Advanced Mathematics

Subtest/ Number of Items	Mean (Standard Deviation)		Percent Correct	
	1970	1981	1970	1981
Part I, 36	11.8 (1.6)	11.1 (1.5)	33	31
Part II, 24	9.0 (1.0)	8.0 (0.9)	38	33

SOURCE: Illinois State Board of Education (1982:42).

TABLE A26 High School and Beyond Mathematics Test Scores, Illinois, Other North Central States, and Total United States

Area	Sophomore Test		Senior Test	
	Mean	Percent Correct	Mean	Percent Correct
Illinois	18.7	49.2	19.2	60.0
Other north central states	19.7	51.8	19.9	62.2
Total United States	18.5	48.7	19.1	59.7

SOURCE: Illinois State Board of Education (1982:43).

"The evidence from the data sources indicates that students preparing to go to college have maintained a plateau with regard to science achievement. However, generally fewer students are exposed to science courses, and as a result, fewer students understand and can apply scientific concepts. The plateau of ACT scores and the drop in the Decade Study results indicate the gulf is also widening among schools in their ability to produce students with a basic knowledge of science."

Michigan

The Michigan Educational Assessment Program (MEAP) is a statewide testing program in reading and mathematics, with other subject areas tested on a sampling basis. The reading and mathematics tests are given to all students in grades 4, 7, and 10. Between 1969 and 1972, standardized, norm-referenced tests were used, but since then Michigan has used state-constructed tests. As curricular objectives change, tests are revised. The current assessment tests were developed in 1980 and are designed to test minimum performance objectives in reading and mathematics. Figure A3 shows performance changes in mathematics with respect to individual schools; Figure A4 shows that females outscore males within the highest range of mathematics attainment.

A science achievement test was administered in 1980 on a sample of students in grades 4, 7 and 10. Results are shown in Table A27. Science performance will be tested again on a sample basis in 1984-1985.

TABLE A27 Cumulative Percentages of Students at Specified Attainment Levels by Grade in the Statewide Sample (Multiple-Choice Only)

	Attainment Levels		
Grade	A	B	C
4	98	92	82
7	97	89	66
10	91	74	50

NOTE: Attainment Level A includes all students who attained 25 percent or more of the objectives at their grade level. Attainment Level B includes those students attaining 50 percent or more of the objectives. Attainment Level C includes those students attaining 75 percent or more of the objectives.

SOURCE: Michigan State Board of Education (1981:49).

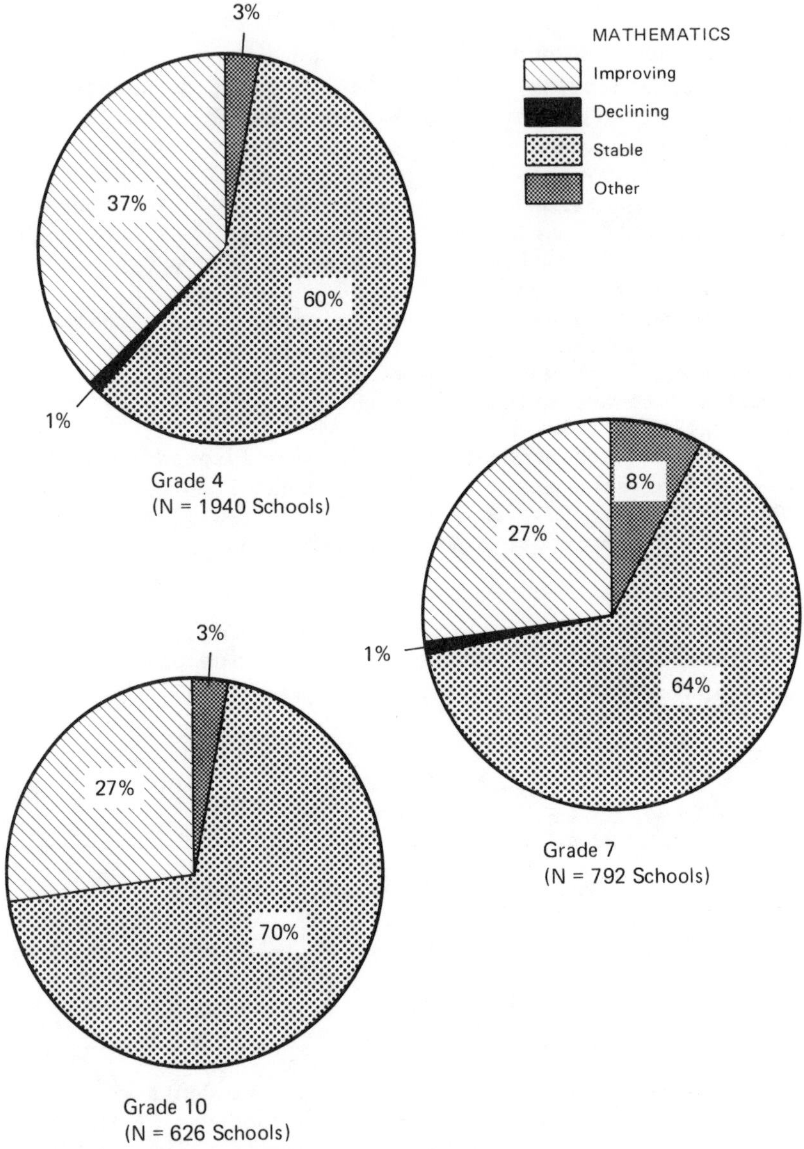

FIGURE A3 Performance changes in mathematics, Michigan schools, 1981-1983.

NOTE: Percentages may not add to 100 because of rounding.

SOURCE: Michigan Board of Education (1984).

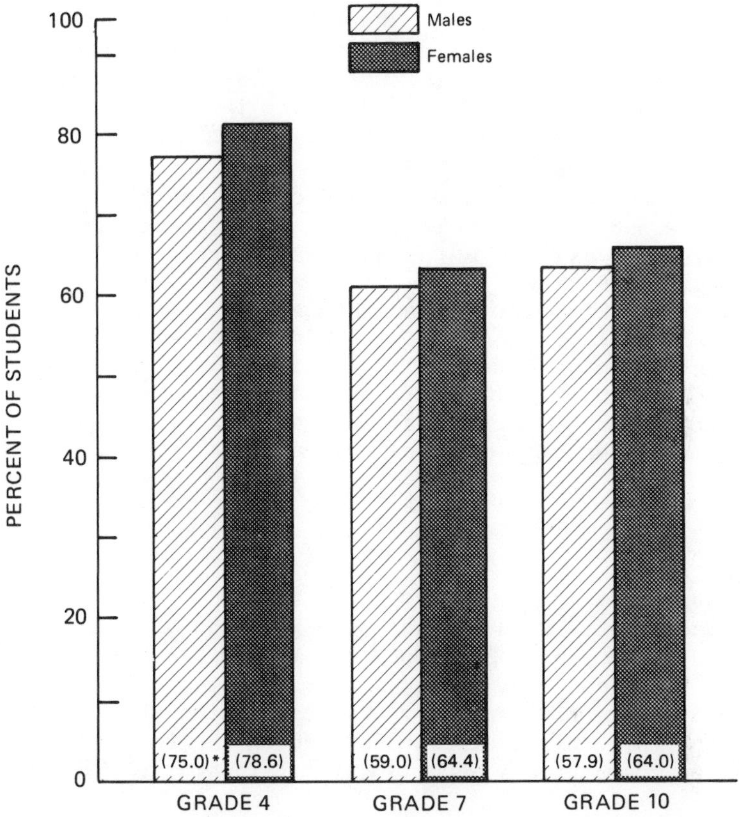

FIGURE A4 1983-1984 mathematics attainment for males and females: Percent of students attaining 75 percent or more of test objectives.

NOTE: Statewide averages for 1982-1983 in parentheses.

SOURCE: Michigan State Board of Education.

Minnesota

Minnesota is using the NAEP as a basis for its assessment program. During a 4-year cycle, 12 different subjects are assessed, 3 per year. An extended NAEP sample of students in grades 4, 8, and 11 is used; half the districts in the state have extended the testing further to include all students in these grades. The NAEP test items are used; for additional subjects, the state adds its own items. The intent is to hold a sufficient number of items constant in order to have a 12-year comparison period. For example, a comparison of performance on identical items in the 1974 and 1978 mathematics tests showed that there was a small overall increase in 1978 in grade 4 (1.2 percent more items answered correctly) and a small decrease in 1978 in grades 8 and 11 (1.3 percent fewer items answered correctly in each grade) (Minnesota Department of Education, 1980a).

Use of NAEP test items and student samples also makes possible comparisons of the performance of Minnesota students with national and regional results. As Table A28 shows, in 1978 Minnesota students performed somewhat better than regional and national samples of students in mathematics and about the same in science.

New Jersey

Since 1978 the New Jersey College Basic Skills Placement Test (NJCBSPT) has been required of all students entering public colleges in New Jersey; as of 1982, 10 independent colleges in New Jersey had also joined the testing program. Table A29 gives the results for the three basic skills assessed in the test: verbal skills, computation, and elementary algebra. As indi-

TABLE A28 1978 Minnesota and National Comparisons in Mathematics and Science Performance, Grades 4, 8, and 11

	Overall Percent Correct, NAEP Items		
	Grade 4	Grade 8	Grade 11
Mathematics			
Minnesota	75.6	60.4	63.6
National	70.0	56.1	59.8
Central United States	73.0	59.6	62.1
Science			
Minnesota	66.7	58.5	50.5
National	63.0	59.7	50.0
Central United States	65.9	61.7	50.3

SOURCE: Minnesota Department of Education (1980a,b).

TABLE A29 Comparison of Statewide Results of High School Graduates Who Took the NJCBSPT, 1978-1982

	1978		1979		1980		1981		1982	
	Number	Percent	Number	Percent	Number	Percent	Number	Percent	Number	Percent
Verbal										
Lack proficiency	7,866	27	7,970	27	7,694	26	8,569	28	8,066	26
Lack proficiency in some areas	12,681	44	12,847	43	12,837	44	13,251	44	14,038	45
Appear to be proficient	8,253	29	9,033	30	8,724	30	8,668	28	9,004	29
Computation										
Lack proficiency[a]	9,915	34	11,793	39	9,255	37	11,589	38	12,398	39
Lack proficiency in some areas	7,596	26	7,477	25	6,654	27	8,210	27	7,500	23
Appear to be proficient	11,335	39	10,673	36	8,922	36	10,741	35	12,066	38
Elementary algebra										
Lack proficiency[a]	14,453	50	14,804	49	12,260	49	15,396	50	16,031	50
Lack proficiency in some areas	10,184	35	10,520	35	9,027	36	10,662	35	11,411	36
Appear to be proficient	4,209	15	4,619	15	3,544	14	4,482	15	4,522	14

[a]Includes those students not attempting this portion of the test.

SOURCE: Advisory Council on Math/Science Teacher Supply and Demand (1983).

cated, there has been little change in results over the 5 years: nearly 40 percent of the students entering the participating colleges lack proficiency computation, and 50 percent lack proficiency in elementary algebra. Moreover, even students who had completed 3 years of high school mathematics (algebra I, geometry, and algebra II) did not fare well: half of these students could not answer 50 percent of the algebra problems presented, and 36 percent of the same students lacked proficiency in 6th-grade arithmetic (defined as answering correctly 20 of the 30 problems presented). Thus, while there is a correlation between the number of mathematics courses taken and performance in the NJCBSPT, the completion of high school mathematics courses does not necessarily lead to proficiency in mathematics (Advisory Council on Math/Science Teacher Supply and Demand, 1983).

New York

At the elementary level, mathematics and reading are tested in grades 3 and 6; in the future, the mathematics test will include computer-related items. Writing is tested in grade 5; the state plans to add tests in social studies and in science to be administered at the end of grade 6. At the secondary level, the Board of Regents exams that test achievement in specific subjects are optional, but they are intended to guide the curriculum in all schools. About three-fourths of the students who take the Regents exams in various levels of mathematics pass the tests; more than 80 percent do so in the sciences (biology, earth science, chemistry, physics). Although scores on Regents exams are not comparable from year to year, the data show that the percentage of students passing the exam in three of the four sciences--biology, earth science, chemistry--has gone up since 1975. However, the numbers of students taking the exams in each of these sciences have decreased slightly. In physics, the percentage passing has remained stable, even though the number of students taking the physics exam has increased by 16 percent in spite of declining total high school enrollments. The percentage passing the various Regents exams in mathematics has remained stable or increased slightly. In 1983, 45 percent of the 194,128 students receiving diplomas in New York received Regents diplomas (University of the State of New York/The State Department of Education, 1983b).

State examinations are also prepared for non-Regents courses in several science subjects and mathematics as well as tests for minimum competency in mathematics, reading, and writing. The minimum-competency tests are first administered in the 8th and 9th grades to identify students needing remediation, then in the middle of 10th grade to ensure students' readiness for graduation. Only 1 percent of diploma candidates fail to graduate because of failure to pass the competency exams.

North Carolina

Statewide assessments have been carried out in mathematics (and other basic subjects) in North Carolina since 1978, in grades 1, 2, 3, 6, and 9. The California Achievement Test (CAT) is used for grades 3, 6, and 9; the Diagnostic Mathematics Inventory (DMI) is used for grades 1 and 2. The results for mathematics are presented in Table A30. Science performance was tested in grade 3 in 1973-1974, in grade 6 in 1974-1975, and in grade 9 in 1975-1976.

Pennsylvania

Pennsylvania's Educational Quality Assessment (EQA) was designed to help local districts improve their educational programs by providing schools with information about the knowledge, skills, and attitudes of their students. Eight cognitive areas, including mathematics, are tested each year in grades 5, 8, and 11. Local school districts volunteer to participate; the number of schools involved has increased considerably since 1978 when the tests were first given; in 1983 more than 1,000 schools participated. Despite the fact that the test population may be changing from year to year, with Philadelphia and Pittsburgh sometimes included and sometimes not, mathematics scores have stayed quite stable over the 6 years that EQA has operated: for grade 5, the mean score every year has been 37 (of 60; standard deviation around 4); for grade 8, 32 (of 60; standard deviation 3.3 to 4.7); for grade 11, 35 (of 60; standard deviation around 3).

TABLE A30 Mathematics Achievement Results and Differences in Performance Between 1979-1980 and 1982-1983

Grade	1979-1980	1980-1981	1981-1982	1982-1983	Gain, 1979-1983
1 (DMI)	2.2	2.3	2.4	2.4	0.2
2 (DMI)	3.3	3.4	3.5	3.5	0.2
3 (CAT)	3.9	4.0	4.1	4.1	0.2
6 (CAT)	6.9	7.3	7.5	7.5	0.6
9 (CAT)	9.4	9.9	10.0	10.0	0.6

NOTE: Results are presented as grade equivalents; national averages equal the seventh month of each grade level. The grade equivalents for grades 1 and 2 are estimates based on linking DMI results to CAT scores.

SOURCE: North Carolina Department of Public Instruction (1983:6).

Washington

Washington has had a statewide testing program since 1975. For the first 3 years, the Comprehensive Tests of Basic Skills (CTBS) were used; in 1979, a change was made to the California Achievement Test (CAT). Table A31 presents results for 7 years. The state also administers the Washington Pre-College test; each year, about 28,000 students (more than 50 percent of each cohort) take this test.

TABLE A31 Comparison of Median Percentile Rank (MPR) in Mathematics Achievement and Percentages of 4th Grade Students Scoring in Each Norm Group Quarter

Norm (%)	1976	1977	1978	1979	1980	1981	1982
25 (top) quartile)	24%	23%	25%	27%	29%	28%	29%
25	25	25	26	28	29	29	29
25	31	32	31	26	26	27	26
25 (bottom quartile)	20	21	17	19	16	17	16
MPR	53	52	54	54	58	56	57

NOTE: The median percentile ranks (MPR's) for the 1976-1978 CTBS have been converted to their CAT equivalents.

SOURCE: Data made available by Washington State Superintendent of Public Instruction, Olympia, Washington.

REFERENCES

Advisory Council on Math/Science Teacher Supply and Demand
1983 Report to the Advisory Council on Math/Science Teacher Supply and Demand. Trenton, N.J.: Department of Higher Education and Department of Education.

Anderson, Beverly
1984 Status of State Assessment and Minimum Competency Testing. Denver, Colo.: Education Commission of the States.

Bell, Terrell H.
1984 State Education Statistics: State Performance Outcomes, Resource Inputs, and Population Characteristics, 1972 and 1982. Washington, D.C.: U.S. Department of Education.

Brouillet, Frank B.
1982 Washington High School Course Enrollment Study: A Focus on Grades 9-12. Tumwater, Wash.: Superintendent of Public Instruction.

Brouillet, Frank B., Rasp, Alfred Jr., and Ensign, Gordon B.

1982 Washington High School and Beyond: A Profile of the 1980 Senior Class. Olympia, Wash.: Superintendent of Public Instruction.

The College Board

1983 Readability Report, Academic Year 1983-84. New York: College Entrance Examination Board.

Council of Chief State School Officers

1982 An Information Exchange on the Status of Statistical and Automated Information Systems in State Education Agencies. A joint product of the National Center for Education Statistics and the Council of Chief State School Officers, Commission on Evaluation of Information Systems, Washington, D.C.

1984 A Review and Profile of State Assessment and Minimum Competency Testing Programs. Prepared for meeting of Chief State School Officers, August 1984.

Dorwart, James P.

1983 Science and Mathematics Teacher Supply and Demand and Educational Needs Analysis: A Pennsylvania Report. Harrisburg: Pennsylvania Department of Education.

Flakus-Mosqueda, Patricia

1983 Survey of States' Teacher Policies. Working Paper No. 2. Prepared for the Education Commission of the States, Denver, Colo.

Hirsch, Christian

1982 Preparedness of Junior High School Mathematics Teachers. Memorandum to NCTM Executive Board. Michigan Council of Teachers of Mathematics, Lansing.

1983 Preparedness of Junior High School Mathematics Teachers. Updated Memorandum to NCTM Executive Board. Michigan Council of Teachers of Mathematics, Lansing.

Howe, Trevor G., and Gerlovich, Jack A.

1982 National Study of the Estimated Supply and Demand of Secondary Science and Mathematics Teachers. Ames: Iowa State University.

Illinois State Board of Education

1980a Special Report on Mathematics. Springfield: Illinois State Board of Education.

1980b Special Report on Science. Springfield: Illinois State Board of Education.

1981 High School and Beyond: An Overview of Illinois Students. Springfield: Illinois State Board of Education.

1982 Student Achievement in Illinois: An Analysis of Student Progress. Springfield: Illinois State Board of Education.

1983 The Supply and Demand for Illinois Mathematics and Science Teachers. Springfield: Illinois State Board of Education.

Laverty, Grace E.

1983 Investigating Mathematics and Science Teacher Supply and Demand in Pennsylvania; A Synthesis of PDE Data. Harrisburg: Pennsylvania Department of Education.

Law, Alexander I.

1984 Student achievement in California schools. In 1982-1983 Annual Report. Sacramento: California State Department of Education.

Michigan Department of Education

1983 Highlights of High School Commission's Survey, 1983. Lansing: Michigan Department of Education.

Michigan State Board of Education

1981 Science Education Interpretive Report. Lansing: Michigan State Board of Education.

1984 Results from the 1983-84 Michigan Educational Assessment Program. Presented to the Michigan State Board of Education, Lansing.

Minnesota Department of Education

1980a Minnesota Statewide Educational Assessment in Mathematics, 1978-79. St. Paul: Minnesota Department of Education.

1980b Minnesota Statewide Educational Assessment in Science, 1978-79. St. Paul: Minnesota Department of Education.

1984 Report of the 1983 Minnesota Survey of Science Education. St. Paul: Minnesota Department of Education.

National Center for Education Statistics

1981 A Capsule Description of High School Students: A Report on High School and Beyond, A National Longitudinal Study for the 1980s. Prepared by Samuel S. Peng, William B. Fetters, and Andrew J. Kolstad. Supt. of Doc. No. NCES 0-729-575/2100. Available from the U.S. Government Printing Office. Washington, D.C.: U.S. Department of Education.

National Evaluation Systems, Inc.
1980 <u>Connecticut Assessment of Educational Progress: Science 1979-80</u>. Prepared for Connecticut State Board of Education, Bureau of Research, Planning and Evaluation. Hartford: Connecticut State Board of Education.

North Carolina Department of Public Instruction
1983 <u>Report of Student Performance</u>. Raleigh: North Carolina Department of Public Instruction.

Roeber, Edward D.
1984 <u>Survey of Large-Scale Assessment Programs, Fall 1983</u>. Lansing: Michigan State Board of Education.

University of the State of New York/The State Education Department
1982 <u>High School and Beyond: A National Longitudinal Study for the 1980's</u>. Report No. 1, A Description of High School Students in New York State and the Nation, 1980. Albany, N.Y.: State Education Department Information Center on Education.
1983a <u>Public School Professional Personnel Report, New York 1982-1983</u>. Albany, N.Y.: State Education Department Information Center on Education.
1983b <u>Regents Examination, Regents Competency Test, and High School Graduation Statistics for the 1982-83 School Year</u>. Albany, N.Y.: Bureau of Elementary and Secondary Testing Programs.
1983c <u>Teachers in New York State, 1968 to 1982</u>. Albany, N.Y.: State Education Department Information Center on Education.

Weiss, Iris S.
1978 <u>Report of the 1977 National Survey of Science, Mathematics, and Social Studies Education</u>. Prepared for the National Science Foundation. Supt. of Doc. No. 083-000-00364-0. Available from the U.S. Government Printing Office. Washington, D.C.: National Science Foundation.

Wolfe, Martin S.
1980 <u>Connecticut Assessment of Educational Progress: Mathematics 1979-80</u>. Prepared for Connecticut State Board of Education, Bureau of Research, Planning and Evaluation. Hartford: Connecticut State Board of Education.

STATE PERSONNEL

California

ALEX LAW, Chief, Planning, Evaluation and Research, California State Department of Education

MARK FETLER, Coordinator, Educational Planning and Information Center, California State Department of Education

CLAIRE QUINLAN, Consultant, Division of Planning, Evaluation, and Research, California State Department of Education

Connecticut

PASCAL D. FORGIONE, Chief, Bureau of Research, Planning and Evaluation, Connecticut State Department of Education

JOAN BARON, Project Director, Connecticut Assessment of Educational Progress

Illinois

MERV BRENNAN, Program Evaluation and Assessment Specialist, Illinois State Board of Education

NORMAL STENZEL, Program Evaluation and Assessment Specialist, Illinois State Board of Education

Michigan

DAVID L. DONOVAN, Assistant Superintendent, Technical Assistance and Evaluation, Michigan State Department of Education

EDWARD D. ROEBER, Supervisor, Michigan Educational Assessment Program, Michigan State Department of Education

Minnesota

LOWELL TORNQUIST, Director, Planning and Policy Research, Minnesota State Department of Education

RICHARD C. CLARK, Specialist, Science Education, Minnesota Department of Education

New Jersey

CONSTANCE O'DEA, Education and Program Specialist, New Jersey State Department of Education

New York

JOHN MURPHY, Assistant Commissioner, Office of Elementary/Secondary and Continuing Support Services, New York State Education Department

JOHN J. STIGLMEIER, Director, Information Center for Education, New York State Education Department

North Carolina

WILLIAM BROWN, Special Assistant for Research, North Carolina Department of Public Instruction

Pennsylvania

ROBERT BURROWS, Educational Statistical Associate, Pennsylvania Department of Education,

J. ROBERT COLDIRON, Chief, Division of Educational Testing and Evaluation, Pennsylvania Department of Education

RICHARD LATTANZIO, Educational Statistical Supervisor, Pennsylvania Department of Education

JOHN J. McDERMITT, Senior Science Advisor, Pennsylvania Department of Education

JOHN A. REBERT, Director, Professional Standards and Practices Commission, Pennsylvania Department of Education

Washington

ALFRED RASP, Director, Testing, Evaluation and Accounting, Washington State Department of Public Instruction